SLOW FOOD

◆

SLOW FOOD

Flavors and Memories of America's Hometowns

◆

MICHAEL JAMES

WARNER BOOKS

A Time Warner Company

Author's Note

I wish to emphasize that while two chapters in this book—
"The Wyoming" and "Praying to the Salmon Spirit"—make
reference to the preparation of game animals, those pages are
included in the spirit of recalling the tradition of necessary
sustenance derived from the land. No endorsement of sport
hunting, which I deplore, is intended or implied.

■■

Warner Books, Inc., 1271 Avenue of the Americas,
New York, New York 10020

W A Time Warner Company

Printed in the United States of America
First printing: May 1992
10 9 8 7 6 5 4 3 2 1

Library of Congress Cataloging-in-Publication Data

James, Michael, 1950–
    Slow food : flavors and memories of America's hometowns / by
Michael James.
        p.   cm.
    Includes index.
    ISBN 0-446-51577-9
    1. Cookery, American.   I. Title.
TX715.J26   1992
641.5973—dc20

91-50403
CIP

Book design by Giorgetta Bell McRee

To James Vlamis and Nancy MacBride Vlamis,
loving parents who raised me to know
good people and good food.

CONTENTS

Slow Food

◆

INTRODUCTION

Slow food is food that's not in a hurry.

It's not so much food that's slow to cook, as food that is worth waiting for. Slow food is the opposite of fast food, cooked at home in small quantities for people you know and love.

This book is about that kind of food and the lives that go with it. It's a book about hometowns, not big towns; about people, not populations; about remembered times, not modern times. And it is a personal book, not a historical one, most often about childhood and the food memories that were stirred into early life. Most especially, this is not a book about fashion, but about American family in all its forms.

Slow food is about seasons. It's about waiting for things to be ripe and finding contentment in the wait like David Beckwith did, propped up under the buckeye trees of his backyard in Davenport, Iowa, watching the tomatoes, big as softballs, swell on his dad's vines. It's about the first sweet North Fork corn coming across Long Island Sound to Bridgehampton to bake in a lobster potpie, and it's about the wild blackberries of August up on the North Yuba River in the Sierras going into a buttery blackberry syrup for Winnie McCrindle's watery pancakes.

Slow food is also the food of comfort: the fried chicken salad and ham biscuits that in 1963 Patsy Cline's mom smuggled into a

1

Seventh Day Adventist hospital in Nashville to restore her injured daughter's spirits.

And it's the food of neighborliness: newlywed Marion Cunningham down in San Diego in the 1940's pumping gas at the Union Oil station in the morning, pumping her new neighbors for recipes in the afternoon, and putting pork chops with marjoram and pineapple dressing on the table at night for her Navy husband Robert. Slow food is good food that brings people closer.

On these pages you will find stories and recipes of American places. Sometimes the stories are about people arriving—the young wine chemist André Tchelistcheff being squired from Paris to the Napa Valley by the Beaulieu Vineyard in 1938 to shape the future of California wines, and so become one of the heroes of the American West he had revered from afar. Other times the story is of someone departing, as with the eight-year-old Jack Canfield, stifled in Torrington, Wyoming, and dreaming of France and willing himself there.

The food and the recipes are mostly American—whatever *that* means. I think it means they spring out of the soil, out of a season, and especially out of a newcomer's longing for his old-world home or an old-timer's love for his new one. American food is what an American eats in a certain time and place, and considering how restless we are, that means American food changes a lot. The food moves, and grows and shifts, as we do, but it is also attached to regions. Wild persimmons thrive in Waveland, Indiana, so stirred persimmon pudding becomes American. Weird radicchios and lettuces run rampant in Huot, Minnesota, and suddenly they are American. Figs ripening in the fall, as Long Island raspberries fade out, round out a baked raspberry pie and make it even more wonderful, and that becomes American.

Valeria Costeiu, newly arrived in Royal Oak, Michigan, baked her beloved *kefli* cookies at Christmas, but with them she also might have served a warm compote made with cranberries instead of the prunes she used back in Romania. Sarah Cavaliere in Monterey grilled her fish coated with olive oil and bread crumbs just like her family did back in Sicily, but she used Monterey Bay salmon instead of the sardines or snapper of Palermo. Texas Joe went to Hawaii as a Navy quartermaster, ate an artichoke, and, his whole system thrown into high gear, awakened to the Asian cooking of the Islands, then settled in New Orleans, where he cooked Cajun and Asian. All those people, living and cooking and eating in all those places, cooked American.

While this is not formally a regional food book (nor is it strictly a cookbook), most mainland regions are represented, starting on the East Coast and moving gradually West, first through the South and Deep South and Texas, then swinging up to the Midwest and Great Lakes states, passing through the Great Plains, pausing in the Northwest and then traveling up through California to the High Sierras, which is a childhood home for me and where the journey ends. While I have naturally dwelt more or less equally on both coasts (with perhaps a bit more emphasis on California, which is, after all, my home), I seem to have markedly dwelt in the Great Lakes and Midwest states. I have a deep respect for the uncluttered quality of life in those places. Especially now, when coastal life is giddy, and even my dearly loved California is becoming cluttered, the good-hearted instincts of the country's middle—no wonder it's called the heartland—are increasingly embraceable. As you progress through these pages I hope you also will have a sense of journey, of scenes anticipated, passing by and passed.

Why am I drawn to all this, you might ask. I have asked myself the same question. After all, I grew up in Berkeley, California, a pretty atypical American place; majored in French, lived in France and spent ten years of my life utterly absorbed by an apprenticeship in French cooking. So it's reasonable to ask: Why does he like American food, and moreover, what does *he* know about it? The answer is simple. It's *because* of France and French food that I love American food. I've returned home, that's all. My wanderlust and my fascination with France, which began when I was fourteen, were fulfilled by the time I was thirty, and I began yearning for the things of home. Weary of sophistication, I craved native life, nearness to family, familiar places. And familiar food. And France, which taught me how good food can be, in the process also taught me how good American food can be. Especially, France taught me about the integrity of ingredients, which is what good food anywhere is based on, and what the food in this book is based on.

Don't look in this book, by the way, for any newfangled food; you won't find it. Most of it is familiar American home cooking, made personal through the presence of home cooks working with local ingredients—Grandmother McNutt coating fresh morels with cracker crumbs and frying them in butter in Waveland, Indiana; Gagi whipping up her wild huckleberry waffles and warm berry jam in Neahkahnie, Oregon; the very French Simca simmering her renowned ducks in red wine in the Napa Valley and finding that the local American Cabernets make the dish as beautiful as the royal Château Margaux of France.

The recipes included on these pages are true to the people and places that provided or inspired them. I have worked to keep them authentic, while making them practical to make and appealing to eat; they are frequently enlightened through simple doses of restraint. The recipes from Wallis Warfield Simpson, for instance, come from a book she compiled in the early 1950's, and while all the tastes she created in her recipes remain, I have enhanced them, I hope, by diminishing the substantial amounts of cream and butter, which, in large amounts, can make food uncomfortable to eat and rather bland. Where instructions were rudimentary or obscure, as with, for example, Dot Snell's gumbo, I have expanded and clarified the recipe. So while the recipes may appear in my style, the flavors and textures of the food come directly from the sources, or are greatly inspired by them. I guess I have acted as a medium, allowing the food to filter through my own experiences and tastes, while knowing that any good cook reading this book will do the same.

While the text and format of most of the recipes are my own, in some cases I have left a recipe, because of what it evokes of its origins, partially or entirely in its original form: the charm or humor or good sense of it would otherwise be lost. The succotash soup falls somewhat into that category, as does the elk chili (with its 2⅛ cups of chopped onion), Gram Murphy's chocolate pie, and the bear stew for 4,000.

A word on salt: I have rarely called for exact quantities of salt or pepper in recipes. Seasoning is a very personal thing, and I have usually left amounts up to the reader (the only exception is where small amounts of salt are present in a dessert preparation). In many recipes where bacon drippings would ordinarily be called for, I have suggested the use of olive oil, which, while not typically American, like bacon fat gives character to the food often associated with warm places while not weighing it down.

Of all the chefs and cooks I have known and worked with, I have had two heroes who were men: the magnificent swashbuckling late Jean Troisgros of Roanne in France who taught me depth in cooking; and Michel Guérard, a fiercely brilliant thinker, who taught me delicacy. Curiously (for a male French chef), Michel also taught me enormous respect for what he called *la cuisine de femme*, the cooking that women do. And I guess that has been the greatest influence on my own cooking, summed up in the one and only Simca (Simone Beck, the mythical French cookbook author) who befriended me in 1971 and changed the course of my life—and who, among other things, baked wonderful cakes. I have always loved women who bake cakes, starting with my mom who always made her own mother's Annette dump cake, and then with Beulah Rogers, my family's housekeeper in Berkeley who taught me to make my own first cake (with blue frosting, I always wanted blue frosting) when I was eight. . . . It's not surprising, then, that the cakes found throughout this book all bear women's names. Kate Bradford's lemon jelly cake. Cese Luther's German chocolate cake. Nana Sarah's sponge cake. Anna Muffoletto's chocolate roll. Diane Rollins' fresh applesauce cake. The prominence of these cake women tells you of the prominence of women in this book and also something further of my own experience. So while there are some stories of men in this book, if the pages seem especially devoted to the kitchens of women, it's because, for me, that's where the real slow food is which fills your life with plenty.

1

THE BOARDWALK
NEAR ORIENT POINT

Orient, New York

T here isn't much boardwalk in Orient, Long Island, and what there is you walk over when you enter the Country Store. But when you walk out, carrying your snow cone with the ice made fresh, the boardwalk is there for a comfortable sit while you work on the cone. Over to the left is the house with the yellow roses, and everywhere a stillness that is the essence of summer in the town.

People who like calm summer like the North Fork of Eastern Long Island. When the big heat months of July and August hit, and the rest of the island is concocting its usual frenzy, you'll find the North Fork dozing. Saturdays and Sundays, sure, the rpm's rise on the main roads, but with just a turn of the wheel you can head down a side road and find yourself a quiet cornfield. Native South Fork people, numbed by the hustle of those Hampton places, gaze over the water to the north and see a kind of haven. The corn is greener and sweeter—isn't it? It always seems so.

On this early September day in the summer of 1988, a friend has called. We're going boating. So Blanca and Babbu—two dogs, mostly white and mostly Labrador—and I pile into the car and race for the northern crossing. There are, actually, two crossings. The first car-ferry carries us from the South Fork to Shelter Island. Off the boat, we drive awhile through dappled woods, then reach the next channel and the ferry for Greenport. In Greenport we take on supplies for the picnic—soft-shell crab sandwiches from the Chow-der Pot Pub. Crunchy and sweet, they are one of the delicacies of a Long Island summer. The next stop is in Orient for a snow cone. Shaded on the rough planks, I suck on the sweet ice and soak up the silence. Blanca gives a lick to the handsome boy husky in the sideyard before we move on.

By the time we get to Peter Manning's house in East Marion it's well on to lunchtime, and Peter, his chums George and Dodie, and the dogs and I all march briskly to the boats. Peter's is a compact troller, no frills, but it gives us a steady glide through the shallows past the slips and onto the clear stretches of the Sound. The motor increases from its steady sputter to a drone. Blanca and Babbu, positioned for ballast, sit peaceably and monitor the spray. Before long we are nosing our way up to the shore of the lonely peninsula of Long Beach. It is not a place of easy pleasures. There is a hard chilling wind, and the beach has only rocks to sit on. There is not a soul in sight. The only motion, down a ways, is the fluttering of beach grass, which looks worrisome to me. The deer tick peril of recent Long Island summers is in full swing again in the summer of '88: men, women and dogs, Lyme disease is stalking us all. So the four of us form a wind break with our backs, huddling at the thin tip of land, spread out our lunch and some good conversation with it and spend a happy couple of hours. After all we are New Yorkers, and know that nothing undoes the presence of rough surroundings like good fellowship.

We have a very tasty lunch. The crab sandwiches have softened a little with the journey, the flavors are blurred and warm. There are tomato sandwiches too, made with local beauties. Dodie has brought along her various homemade pickles, which make me stop in the middle of a mouthful. They are some of the most delicious and delicate things I have ever eaten. I eat bread-and-butter pickles and old-fashioned dill pickles during lunch and on into dessert: The pickles even taste good with raspberries. I can't decide which kind is best. I taste one, then the other, while the sun sears us and on our desolate perch we feel the fullness of summer around us.

After a while, craving shade, we pile back into the boat and push away from Long Beach. The lawns and old trees of East Marion are motionless and soothing after the restless heat of the Sound. We have tall drinks and become easy again and, before you know it, hungry again. In the twilight we drive off to a local place and cram into a booth for pizza and beer. Finally Blanca and Babbu and I begin the journey home, heading south into the night, across the channels, on and off the ferries, gathered up by the woods of Shelter Island, then released again, moving home, two worn-out dogs in the back, quiet in the rushing night, dreaming of the day's sun.

THE BOARDWALK
NEAR ORIENT POINT

Dodie's Old-Fashioned Dill Pickles
and Easy Bread-and-Butter Pickles

Wedges of Iceberg with White Cheddar
and Chive Dressing

Long Island Lobster Potpie,
with Corn and Cabernet

Baked Raspberries and Figs

Angel Food Cake

My first Long Island summer I spent out in the dunes near the potato fields of Bridgehampton. The house was gray and looked like a small ferryboat come ashore. The curves of the decks and the railings and the views of Mecox Bay made you feel pretty nautical. The kitchen overlooked the other upstairs rooms and the shore views to the east and some tasty cooking came out of it that summer. The favorite dinner was a grilled lobster feed. On Wednesdays, Wainscott Fish sold lobsters five for $20. One friend or another could make the afternoon pickup, while someone else lit the charcoal and chopped the garlic for the basting butter, and someone else shucked the corn and I made the pie. However, when guests were coming and it wasn't Wednesday, I often made a lobster potpie. It only required two lobsters to feed six, and yet it was a generous dish, and as it evolved over that summer it kept acquiring new flavors. Long Island corn is one of the world's delicacies and eventually it seemed only natural to add it to the pie. If you have more mature, less tender corn on the day you make this dish, you may want to consider cooking the corn kernels in a little butter and milk first to make them tender before adding them to the lobster. The presence of red wine with lobster may at first seem startling, but actually it gives a certain strength to the flavors and balances the sweetness of lobster and corn.

Wonderful things grow on Eastern Long Island, and if they ever stop building houses there, hopefully some farms will survive. One of the lettuces I grew fond of they call French iceberg. I don't know why it was French, I guess the outer leaves had a few more frills, but inside it was crisp and juicy just like plain iceberg. Much maligned nowadays, iceberg is an honorable lettuce, if you give it fair treatment. If it's fresh and cold and served with a creamy, *unsweet* homemade dressing, it is one of the great things to eat. That Bridgehampton summer we always served it first, and enjoyed it on its own.

Fruit pies were always the desserts of Long Island summer. Hardly a morning went by that either my pal Sandy or I didn't have that rolling pin out by nine. We practiced our lattice tops, but just as often laid a full layer of dough over the pie because everyone clamored for more crust. Blanca and Babbu even concurred. One afternoon we trooped in from the beach and found two dog snouts dyed cherry red: The pups had feasted on still-hot Bing cherry pie. When we could get them, North Fork raspberries also went into a pie. Baked raspberry pie beats a cream pie any day. Sometimes, when I wanted a softer flavor, I would add figs, whose sweetness and earthiness mellowed the berries. It is an unusual, lavish kind of pie, and even when the filling is baked without the crust and served after a savory pie such as lobster, it is every bit as satisfying. With this baked fruit dessert, tender, damp slices of homemade vanilla angel food cake are just right. I used to dismiss angel food cake, until I started baking it myself. Now I know this plain dessert is one of the most beautiful.

About Dodie's pickles . . . you be the judge. Are they really as good to eat with raspberries as I remember? Are they even perfect with lobster? You decide.

DODIE'S OLD-FASHIONED DILL PICKLES

For 2 dozen

1 cup cider vinegar
5 cups water
½ cup coarse salt
24 small (3 to 4 inches) cucumbers, rinsed
15 to 18 fresh dill tops, gone to seed, or 2½ to 3 teaspoons dill
    seed
25 to 30 whole peppercorns

Combine the vinegar, water and salt in a medium nonaluminum saucepan. Bring to the boil, stirring occasionally to dissolve the salt, and remove from the heat. Cool 10 minutes. Divide the cucumbers among 5 or 6 sterilized pint jars. Add 3 dill tops with the seeds, or ½ teaspoon dill seed, and 5 peppercorns to each jar. Pour enough of the vinegar mixture into each jar to cover the cucumbers. Seal the jars with the lids. Place in a simmering hot water bath for 10 minutes. Cool upside down. Let the pickles stand at least 6 weeks before serving. Serve well chilled.

DODIE'S EASY BREAD-AND-BUTTER PICKLES

Makes 7 cups

6 cups (about 2½ pounds) thinly sliced unpeeled cucumbers
1 medium onion, peeled and sliced
1½ cups white wine vinegar
1½ cups sugar
½ teaspoon ground turmeric
½ teaspoon salt
½ teaspoon mustard seed
½ teaspoon celery seed

Layer the cucumbers and onion in a large glass bowl or dish. Combine the remaining ingredients in a small nonaluminum saucepan and bring to the boil, swirling the pan occasionally until the sugar is dissolved. Pour the mixture over the cucumbers and onion; allow to cool. Cover tightly with plastic wrap and refrigerate for 24 hours.

The pickles will keep for up to 1 month in the refrigerator, or they can be canned using the water-bath method and processing the jars for 10 minutes (see preceding recipe for dill pickles).

WEDGES OF ICEBERG WITH WHITE CHEDDAR AND CHIVE DRESSING

■■

Serves 6 (approximately 2 cups of dressing)

1 cup olive oil
2 teaspoons white wine vinegar
2 tablespoons lemon juice
4 ounces aged white cheddar cheese, broken into 5 or 6 pieces
¼ cup sour cream
1 teaspoon salt
Freshly ground pepper to taste
5 or 6 fresh chives
10 or 12 fresh basil leaves, rinsed, plus 6 small sprigs of basil
6 generous wedges of iceberg lettuce, freshly sliced
18 small golden tomatoes, washed and sliced in half

Place the oil, vinegar, lemon juice, cheese, sour cream, seasonings, chives and basil leaves in a blender or food processor and blend until well mixed and the herbs are chopped. Do not overmix—the dressing should retain some lumps of cheddar. Correct the seasoning with salt and pepper. If you wish a thinner dressing, add a small amount of water. Serve cool or cold over the wedges of lettuce and garnish with the tomatoes and basil sprigs.

LONG ISLAND LOBSTER POTPIE, WITH CORN AND CABERNET

Serves 6

2 1½- to 2-pound live lobsters
2 medium carrots, peeled and finely diced
2 stalks celery, washed thoroughly and diced
1 medium onion, peeled and finely chopped
10 tablespoons light olive oil
1¼ cups Cabernet Sauvignon (or other good red wine)
2 or 3 branches of fresh thyme, or 1 teaspoon dried thyme
    leaves
Small bunch of parsley
1 tomato, coarsely chopped
1 pound fresh fennel, finely sliced
Salt and freshly ground pepper to taste
1 tomato, peeled, seeded and diced
1 tablespoon finely minced shallot
1½ tablespoons flour
1 teaspoon finely chopped fresh tarragon, or ¼ teaspoon dried
    tarragon
1 tablespoon heavy cream
4 ears of raw, sweet corn, shucked, the kernels cut off the cob

For the pastry and egg wash

1 cup unbleached all-purpose flour
¼ teaspoon salt
1 teaspoon baking powder
5 tablespoons unsalted butter
2½ to 3 tablespoons heavy cream
1 egg yolk beaten with 1 tablespoon water

Drop the lobsters into a large quantity of rapidly boiling salted water, cover with a lid and remove from the heat. After 2 or 3 minutes remove the lobsters and allow to cool. Remove all of the lobster meat from the tails, claws and knuckles. Reserve any of the liquid, creamy lobster butter (the fat) and the greenish tomalley (the liver) that accumulates in the process. Crush all of the lobster shells along with the legs and body either in a food processor or with a cleaver (the claws should not go into the processor, but may be chopped by hand).

Stew the carrots, celery and onion in 3 tablespoons of the olive oil over low heat in a large covered casserole, stirring frequently. After about 5 minutes add the chopped lobster shells, stirring together well with the aromatic ingredients. Pour in 1 cup of the red wine and bring to the simmer. Add just enough water to barely cover the contents of the pot; add the fresh thyme, parsley and coarsely chopped tomato. Simmer the broth for about 45 minutes, stirring occasionally. Strain the liquid through a fine sieve into a medium saucepan and reduce over medium-high heat to 1½ cups.

Place 4 tablespoons of the remaining olive oil in a large heavy-bottomed saucepan, add the fennel, and stir over medium-low heat for 3 to 4 minutes. Add the remaining ¼ cup red wine, season lightly with salt and pepper, cover and cook, stirring occasionally, until the fennel is just tender, 15 to 20 minutes.

Warm the 3 remaining tablespoons of the olive oil in a saucepan, add the diced tomato and the minced shallot and cook briefly over medium-low heat. Add the flour and cook for 3 to 4 minutes, stirring constantly. Pour on the reduced lobster broth and whisk steadily as the sauce comes to the boil and thickens. Simmer for 5 minutes, whisking frequently. Stir in the tarragon and the heavy cream; correct the seasoning with salt and pepper.

Combine the sliced lobster tail meat and the rest of the lobster meat with the cooked fennel, the fresh corn kernels and the sauce. Taste for seasoning, then spread evenly in a 12-inch oval baking dish (or a 10-inch glass pie plate). Spoon some of the reserved lobster butter and tomalley, put through a fine sieve, over the lobster meat mixture (any remaining tomalley can be frozen and used to enrich another dish). The dish may be completed in advance up to this point: Cover with plastic wrap and refrigerate. It may now wait for up to a day. Bring to room temperature before proceeding with the recipe.

Preheat the oven to 400° F.

Prepare the pastry: In a small mixing bowl or in a food processor stir together the flour, salt and baking powder. Blend in the butter, then moisten with the heavy cream, adding extra drops as needed to form the dough into a ball. On a lightly floured surface roll out the dough into an oval (or a round) slightly larger than the baking dish you are using. Fold the edges under and crimp to form an attractive standing border. Lay the decorated pastry gently over the baking dish (don't worry if the dough does not completely cover the lobster mixture). Make several slashes in the dough to allow steam to escape; brush thoroughly with the egg wash. Bake the potpie for 25 to 30 minutes, or until the pastry is just done. Do not overbake or the lobster will overcook. Allow to cool on a rack for 10 to 15 minutes before spooning onto warm plates.

BAKED RASPBERRIES AND FIGS

Serves 6

4 ½-pint baskets of raspberries
½ pound fresh figs— black, green or white—peeled and
    quartered
¾ to 1 cup sugar, depending on the sweetness of the berries
1 teaspoon fresh thyme leaves, or ½ teaspoon dried thyme
    leaves (optional)
3 tablespoons butter

Preheat the oven to 400° F.

In a mixing bowl gently stir together the raspberries, figs, sugar and optional thyme leaves. Turn into a 2-quart shallow baking dish; dot with the butter. Bake for 25 to 30 minutes, until the juices are bubbling and the fruit is tender. Serve warm.

Variation (when not served with a main course pie):

RASPBERRY FIG PIE

Add 2 tablespoons flour to the above mixture and turn into a 10-inch pie plate lined with pie dough as directed on page 272. Cover with a top layer of dough or a lattice top and bake.

ANGEL FOOD CAKE

A 10-inch cake for 10 to 12

1 cup sifted cake flour
1¾ cups sifted sugar
½ teaspoon salt
12 eggs whites (approximately 1½ cups) at room temperature
1 tablespoon water
2 teaspoons lemon juice
½ teaspoon vanilla extract
1 teaspoon cream of tartar
Optional frosting for the cake: 1½ cups heavy cream beaten
       with ¼ cup sugar and 1 teaspoon vanilla extract

Preheat the oven to 325° F.
   Sift the flour, ½ cup of the sugar and the salt together 3 times, then return to the sifter.

Using an electric mixer or other reliable beater, whip the egg whites until foamy, then beat in the water, lemon juice, vanilla and cream of tartar. When the whites begin to form soft peaks, gradually add the remaining 1¼ cups sugar, beating until the whites form almost firm peaks. Sift the flour, sugar and salt mixture over the whites and gently fold it in. Pour or spoon the batter into an ungreased 10-inch tube pan (the batter will climb up the dry metal sides when it bakes) and run a flexible-blade spatula through the mixture to distribute it evenly and remove any air pockets. Bake for 45 to 50 minutes. The cake will rise considerably as it bakes, then settle back onto itself slightly as it finishes baking. It is done when the top is a light brown and the edges have begun to pull away from the sides. Do not overbake: The cake should keep a soft and very tender quality.

When the cake is done, if you are using an angel food cake pan immediately invert the pan onto its stubby legs; otherwise invert the pan and suspend the tube over a bottle neck. This clearly peculiar procedure helps the cake retain its airy structure as it cools. When the cake is cool, dislodge it from the pan using a thin spatula and your fingers. Spread with the cream frosting, if desired. The cake is best not sliced, which tends to crush it, but pulled apart into slices with 2 forks. The portions will be uneven but will look, and taste, homemade.

2

....

THE MAHARANI OF
HILLSDALE

Hillsdale, New York

W e arrived late Thursday in Hillsdale, riding among mists, under a phantom moon. Some swore they saw the headless horseman, and Sleepy Hollow seemed over the hill. By the time the farmhouse was lit, the lamb roasted and the corn shucked, it was getting onto one A.M., and that old Ichabod Crane creepiness had left me and the corn tasted sweet and safe.

Friday morning the rains began, the steaming rains of New York autumn. But blueberry pancakes appearing briskly out of the kitchen brightened the sleepy members of the wedding. By evening the tasks were done, the lofty Grange—the 150-year-old former hub of Hillsdale farming families—was newly groomed for the next day's marriage. Great blooms of white hydrangea, gathered on a stealthy operation in the town cemetery, gave companionable curves to the stiffness of pink and purple gladiolas at the great hall's door. The brooks and soggy fields gurgled and sent skyward a collective chant for sun.

The sky heard and Saturday was resplendent, a great crisp September day for a wedding near the Berkshire Mountains. As a hundred guests sat and grew still in the Grange, the ingenuous sun of the New World invaded the hall, pierced the clusters of tall pane glass and filled the room with quiet. And India, bright and sweet and old, was all at once a great deal present—in garlands of cedar and

25

marigolds, in the iridescence of old silk and the weight of family diamonds, in the luminous face of the bride—and as the "thali women" blessed the bride and groom in the pure high song of Mother India and scattered rose petals and rice, the blessings reached us all.

On Sunday, as the Grange was restored to calm and the farmhouse emptied out, the wedding music played over and over in the rooms and in our thoughts, and its serene pulse, like an Indian raga, had the warmth of a steady heart. Richard Robbins composed it for the lovers of Hillsdale, just as he had composed beautiful music for the film lovers of *A Room with a View* and *Maurice*. For Madhur Jaffrey, whose daughter Sakina was married that day, the marriage will be remembered in the music and in other sun-soaked days in Hillsdale, where that one September the Delhi of her youth appeared again and hung in the air around us.

THE MAHARANI OF HILLSDALE

Red Lentil Soup with Cloves

Sunday Leg of Lamb, with Cilantro,
Ginger and Lemon

Beet Stew Kashmiran Rani Style

Crisp Potato Galette

Cold Passion Fruit Soufflé
with Passion Fruit
and Fresh Mint Sauce

———

I met Madhur Jaffrey fifteen years ago, and I think of her as the woman who made me love lentils. Along the way she also made me love India. Before I ever met Madhur I saw her in a James Ivory film called *Autobiography of a Princess*. In the film Madhur the princess serves tea to James Mason, her visitor, and I was smitten as much by the view of India through the eyes of an expatriate princess living in London as by her brewing of a proper pot of tea. When I invited Madhur to California in 1975 to present her in a series of cooking classes, I fetched her at the San Francisco Airport and drove her to a woodsy house in Berkeley, and the first thing she did was brew a perfect pot of tea. She has been a princess to me ever since.

Madhur Jaffrey, a native of New Delhi and now a New Yorker, has three careers. She is an actress, a veteran of many James Ivory films as well as of the London stage. Madhur is also a writer of cookbooks and children's stories. Then she is mother to three grown girls and wife to Sanford Allen, a prominent concert violinist with roots in rural Kentucky. Madhur is unassuming about all of this, and happiest when her life allows her refuge in Hillsdale, where she can be snug with Sanford and a friend or two, cook for them, and then draw up to a fire for a good talk and a chuckle over some Johnnie Walker Black.

When Madhur cooks there are always the clear tastes of India. There is no mongrelization of spices; they may be combined but they never blur and each has a purpose. Madhur often cooks Indiany dishes—French or American with a bit of India added—with Sanford who is a first-rate cook himself. The red lentil soup and the beet stew in the following menu come from Madhur's mother, Kashmiran Rani, and are quite delicate. The variety of lentils found in India have different tastes and so have different specific uses. The red lentils that are frequently used for soups (most often found in this country in health food stores) will actually lose their color as they cook. In Madhur's mother's recipe they end up a mustardy color from the addition of turmeric. Unlike most lentil soups this one is light and almost frothy, gently flavored with clove, and tingling with lime. The beet stew is richly flavored with cumin seeds that roast in oil, and a pinch of ground asafetida. This rather exotic ingredient, which can be found in spice shops, comes from

28

the dried resin of a tree and has a strong, truffly flavor and excellent digestive qualities.

The roasted leg of lamb has some jumpy Caribbean tastes. Madhur calls it "Trinidadian" as she once saw a woman do lamb this way there. The fairly blunt heat of fresh green chile along with garlic and a lavish amount of cracked pepper is streaked with the flavors of ginger, lemon and cilantro—all of which get "shoved," in Madhur's words, into slits in the lamb. The potato accompaniment is really the famous French "Potatoes Anna," done not with butter but with olive oil, and it is just as wonderfully crisp. In season, sweet corn on the cob would go as well with the leg of lamb.

After the many flavors of the lamb dinner, a cold fruit soufflé has a calming effect. If you can find fresh passion fruit, which are ripest when they are wrinkly, their stunning tropical flavor is perfect for this dessert. Failing passion fruit, one cup of fresh lemon juice can be substituted for the orange and passion fruit juices. Since it is based mostly on egg whites, this is not a particularly rich dessert. The addition of beaten cream gives a little body and, rather mysteriously, a slight golden flavor to the fruit. The accompanying fresh mint sauce is refreshing and enhances the flavors too. The crucial thing in this cold soufflé is the use of just the minimum amount of gelatin to make it set and still allow it a fragile quality.

A note on heat: I have been circumspect about the amount of spicy heat in this menu. Cayenne appears as an ingredient in only the lamb and the beets, and I have made it optional both times. The meat is actually already fairly spicy because of the chile flavoring; if you want more heat you can certainly hit the leg with some cayenne (ditto the beets). I personally don't like much heat since it seems to crush other flavors. And, as Madhur reminds us, much Indian cooking is not hot at all.

RED LENTIL SOUP WITH CLOVES

Serves 6

1½ cups red lentils, rinsed and drained
7 cups water
½ teaspoon ground turmeric
6 whole cloves, tied in a small piece of cheesecloth
2 small slices peeled fresh ginger
1 garlic clove, peeled
3 to 4 teaspoons salt
Freshly ground pepper to taste
2 to 3 tablespoons fresh lime juice to taste
½ cup small cubes of unsweet bread
Olive oil
Wedges of fresh lime

Combine the lentils, water, turmeric, cloves, ginger and garlic in a large pot and simmer, partially covered, until the lentils are very soft, about 45 minutes. Remove the cloves, pressing on the cheesecloth to extract all the flavor, and purée the soup in a blender. Season with 3 to 4 teaspoons salt, the pepper, and lime juice to taste.

Sauté the bread cubes in a small amount of olive oil until they are crisp and brown. Drain thoroughly on paper towels. Serve the soup in warmed soup plates with the croûtons and lime wedges on the side.

SUNDAY LEG OF LAMB, WITH CILANTRO, GINGER AND LEMON

Serves 6

6 garlic cloves, peeled
½ cup cilantro leaves, lightly packed in the measure
1½ inches fresh ginger, peeled
1 serrano chile, split and the seeds removed, or other hot fresh
    chile
4 tablespoons finely chopped onion
Juice of 2 lemons
Salt
1 6-pound leg of lamb at room temperature—the fat, "fell"
    (thick skin) and hip bone removed (shank and leg bones
    remain)
Olive oil
2 tablespoons cracked pepper
1/16 teaspoon cayenne (optional)

Preheat the oven to 425° F.

Chop the garlic, cilantro, ginger and chile very fine in a food processor or with a knife. Place in a bowl and add the onion, lemon juice and ½ teaspoon or so of salt. Cut several slits about 1½ inches long and ⅓ inch deep in the lamb and shove in the spicy mixture; save any leftover mixture to use later in the sauce. Salt the lamb, oil it lightly, and encrust with the cracked pepper. If desired, sprinkle with the cayenne. Place the lamb in a large shallow roasting pan and roast it in the oven for about 1 hour for rare lamb, and 1 hour and 10 to 15 minutes for medium-rare meat. Turn the lamb 2 or 3 times as it roasts. When the meat is done set it on a carving board and cover with aluminum foil to keep warm. Allow the lamb to rest for 45 minutes to 1 hour before carving, which will allow the juices to recede into the meat and the muscles to relax, making the meat more tender and juicy when served (and also much easier to carve).

Pour the pan juices from the roasting pan into a glass measure and remove all the fat from the top. Set the roasting pan over low heat, add ½ cup water and scrape up all the coagulated meat juices with a wooden spoon. When the juices have dissolved, pour the liquid into a small saucepan (you may strain it if you wish). Add the reserved, defatted roasting liquid and any leftover spicy mixture. Simmer over low heat until reduced by half. Correct the seasoning with salt and pepper.

Carve the lamb and arrange it on a platter; season the meat lightly. Spoon any of the loose spicy mixture from the roast over and around the meat. Pour over the meat any juices that have accumulated during the carving, spoon over a little sauce and pass the rest on the side.

BEET STEW KASHMIRAN RANI STYLE

Serves 6

2 tablespoons olive oil
½ teaspoon ground asafetida (available in spice shops)
1 teaspoon cumin seeds
½ teaspoon ground turmeric
2½ pounds beets, trimmed, peeled and cut into ½-inch-thick
    wedges—or 3 dozen baby beets, trimmed and peeled
1 cup tomato sauce, preferably homemade or a good-quality
    canned
½ cup water
1½ teaspoons salt
Freshly ground pepper to taste
1/16 teaspoon cayenne (optional)

Heat the oil in a large saucepan set over medium-low heat and add the asafetida, shaking the pan briefly. After a few seconds add the cumin seeds; when they begin to sizzle, add the turmeric, beets, tomato sauce, water and seasonings. Cover and simmer, stirring occasionally, until the beets are just tender, for about 30 to 40 minutes. Don't let the beets become too soft. Uncover and correct the seasoning with salt and pepper. The sauce should be fairly thick; if necessary, reduce it briefly before serving.

CRISP POTATO GALETTE

Serves 6

5 to 6 tablespoons olive oil
2½ pounds Russet potatoes, peeled and cut into ⅛-inch-thick
    slices
Salt and freshly ground pepper
2 teaspoons chopped fresh thyme leaves, or 1 teaspoon dried
    thyme leaves
2 teaspoons chopped fresh rosemary, or ½ teaspoon dried
    rosemary

Preheat the oven to 400° F.

Heat 4 tablespoons of the olive oil in a 12-inch nonstick skillet with an ovenproof handle set over medium heat. Place 1 slightly overlapping layer of potatoes in the skillet, season lightly, sprinkle with some of the herbs and a little additional olive oil, then continue layering the remaining potatoes, adding seasonings, herbs and oil, until all the ingredients are used up. With a large spatula press the entire surface firmly to help the potatoes stick together, cover with a lid or a piece of aluminum foil and bake until the potatoes are tender, about 35 to 40 minutes. Uncover and run the potatoes under a hot broiler to brown them lightly. Unmold onto a warm serving platter. (If you have used a nonstick skillet, the galette should unmold perfectly; if you have used a cast-iron or other skillet and the potatoes are sticking, simply serve them directly from the pan.) Sprinkle with additional herbs if you wish; cut into wedges and serve.

COLD PASSION FRUIT SOUFFLÉ WITH PASSION FRUIT AND FRESH MINT SAUCE

Serves 8 to 10

1 dozen passion fruit
Finely grated rind of 2 oranges
½ cup fresh orange juice
2 cups sugar
2 envelopes powdered gelatin, softened in ½ cup cold water
14 egg whites at room temperature
Pinch of salt
2 cups heavy cream
Sprigs of fresh mint
Powdered sugar in a shaker

Fit a 2-quart soufflé dish with a wax paper or parchment paper collar that extends at least 2 inches above the rim of the dish. Cut the passion fruit in half, scoop out the juicy pulp and strain to remove the seeds; you should have about ½ cup juice. Place the passion fruit juice, orange rind, orange juice and 1 cup sugar in a small heavy-bottomed saucepan, set over medium heat and bring to the simmer. When the sugar has dissolved and the mixture is clear, remove from the heat and stir in the gelatin.

Beat the egg whites with the pinch of salt until they begin to foam. Gradually add the remaining 1 cup sugar, beating the whites at high speed until they form fairly stiff peaks (they should not be dry). Lower the mixer speed to medium-slow and beat in the hot sugar and gelatin mixture. Pour into a large stainless steel bowl and set in the refrigerator to cool, folding the mixture occasionally with a rubber spatula to prevent it from separating as it begins to set.

Beat the heavy cream until stiff. When the meringue mixture is cool, fold in the beaten cream. Pour into the soufflé dish, smooth the top, press a piece of plastic wrap directly onto the surface and refrigerate until ready to serve. Garnish with the mint and dust lightly with the powdered sugar. Spoon onto plates and pass the sauce on the side.

PASSION FRUIT AND FRESH MINT SAUCE

For 1¼ cups

½ cup sugar
½ cup water
6 passion fruit, scooped out and strained to make
approximately ¼ cup juice
2 teaspoons finely chopped fresh mint

Place the sugar, water and passion fruit juice in a small saucepan and bring to the simmer. When the sugar has dissolved and the mixture is clear, remove from the heat and pour into a bowl set over ice water. Add the mint and stir over the ice until the sauce is cold. Cover and refrigerate.

Note: This recipe makes a large 2-quart soufflé serving 8 to 10 people, more than you really *need* for this 6-person menu. You can halve the recipe if you wish, but the presentation will not be as dramatic.

Variation:

COLD LEMON SOUFFLÉ

Substitute 1 cup fresh lemon juice for the passion fruit and orange juices and proceed with the recipe.

3

TANKING OVER ALFRED

Boston, Massachusetts

Around 1950 Avis DeVoto became completely disgusted with kitchen knives. The stainless knives of the era weren't sharp when you bought them and you couldn't sharpen them when they got duller. So there the Cambridge, Massachusetts, literary scout and accomplished home cook was, hacking dully away when her husband Bernard, a prominent historian and political writer, intervened with some slashing commentary in *Harper's* magazine. Bernard DeVoto also frequently championed consumer causes, and he let American knife manufacturers have it. Mail, much of it containing knife samples, poured in from all over the world to the DeVoto house on tame Berkeley Street—for a while Avis felt as if she were stocking an arsenal—including a letter from a Mrs. J. Child in Paris accompanied by a small carbon steel paring knife. Most of the arriving knives were dull and worthless but the Paris knife, which darkened with age but kept a keen edge, was brilliant. That simple message from France to the States was not the last from the J. Child person.

Years passed and the contact between Avis DeVoto and Julia Child grew into a correspondence that deepened into friendship when the Childs paid a first visit to the DeVotos in 1954. Paul Child, who was on a State Department assignment in Paris, had a year's leave of absence and the Childs were decompressing awhile in

Washington, D.C., when they decided to trot up to Cambridge to meet Julia's pen pal. Avis was eager for that first contact; Bernard wasn't, and grumbled about strangers in the house. On a Sunday afternoon, while the DeVotos were having a small cocktail party, a large station wagon pulled up in front of the house loaded to the roof with pots and pans, the whole *batterie de cuisine*. Avis greeted the Childs and drew them into the party. Bernard sniffed. When he couldn't ignore Julia any longer he walked up to her and asked her what she would have to drink, and, as Avis told it, "Julia looked *down* at him because she's a very tall woman and said, 'Well, I think I'll have one of those Martinis I've been reading about.' He had done the famous article about the dry Martini in *Harper's*, and she drank two or three without turning a hair, although she must have felt them. And Benny (Bernard) of course admired that enormously, so his attitude softened a great deal."

The ice broken, the Childs stayed a week. Julia set up shop in the kitchen and cooked for days. She skinned halibut. When the fridge was empty one day she poked around son Mark DeVoto's vegetable patch and produced a tasty main course soup with poached eggs. She baked a French chocolate cake. In between meals Avis and Julia thumbed through the book manuscript that Julia had also jammed into the station wagon. After graduating from the Cordon Bleu cooking school in the late 1940's, Julia had met a French woman named Simone Beck and the two women had begun work on a French cookbook for Americans. After the knife episode, Julia had drawn Avis into the project as an impromptu editor/consultant/ champion, and as Julia and Simca (as Simone Beck's friends knew her) slaved away during the early 1950's, Avis had supplied frequent support. She tested recipes, and she chatted up the book with Houghton Mifflin, a Boston publisher with whom Avis occasionally worked as an editor. Houghton Mifflin, viewing the expanding work, eventually nibbled and offered a contract and a $200 advance in 1954.

Julia and Paul returned to Europe and the work of the three women continued: Simca giving the book the true French taste, Julia transmitting that taste through American ingredients and know-how and Avis keeping a fire lit under Houghton Mifflin, not to mention sometimes acting as referee between the two powerful personalities raging and chortling their way through, among other things, hundreds of pounds of American flour and butter bought at the Paris PX in their search for delectable equivalents of French pastry doughs. At one point, in a dispute over endless changes in a *cassoulet*, Julia was heard to mutter something about "that old goat," and she wasn't referring to stew. The great improvisationalist, Simca, on the other hand often felt fettered by Julia's eternal science of measures, her *sacré* cups. Then there was the recreation of what Mark DeVoto now refers to as the Götterdämmerung of French cooking, Veal Prince Orloff with its page after succulent page of braising and slicing and stuffing and saucing—and one wonders how the collective livers and tempers survived that one. Under the pressures of coauthorship the friendship sometimes strained but it never snapped thanks to Avis's steadying influence and her insistence that the work must go on.

Around 1956 the aspiring authors had a serious setback. Julia journeyed to Boston with 800 pages of chicken under her arm and Houghton Mifflin said NO, we're not going to publish an encyclopedia. Deflated, Julia carried the news home to Simca. From their respective vantage points Avis and Simca cheered Julia up and the book was off and running again. In 1958, this time armed with Simca herself, as well as a revised manuscript, Julia marched once again into the publisher's offices, having journeyed with Simca by Greyhound bus from Washington to Boston in the middle of the night when all the trains were shut down by a blizzard. A little white around the eyes, the women waited for the word from on high. Once again it was NO. A senior editor at Houghton Mifflin, a woman named Dorothy de Santillana, was overcome by the manuscript and dearly wanted it. But the men editors were more interested in a Texas cookbook they had in the works that used a lot of mixes and marshmallows. Stymied, Julia and Simca weighed their options. If marshmallow cooking was more important than their cooking, it was time to shop around. On that deadly winter day in 1958 Simone Beck and Julia Child walked away from Houghton Mifflin and never looked back.

Simca returned to France, Julia to Washington, and Avis was left holding the manuscript. As it happened, she knew right where to go.

For several years Avis had been scouting for Alfred Knopf, had found him quite a few books to publish, which, unfortunately, all lost money and Alfred ultimately said, "Well, we'd better part company," all very friendly and everything. Avis, nonetheless still well connected at Knopf, very smoothly sent the manuscript over to, not Alfred, but Bill Koshland, the Vice President, telling him not to read it but to *cook* with it. Two months of silence and fingernail chewing followed. One night around ten the phone rang at the DeVotos and it was Bill Koshland who said, "Four of us have been cooking with this book, we've cooked our way straight through it and it works and we're going to tank right over the Knopfs." Just bulldoze the boss. People said that Blanche Knopf, Alfred's wife, was an old sourpuss and knew that *her* sister Helen was publishing a cookbook for chauffeurs or something, and that that was all the Knopf bunch was going to care about. So Bill Koshland took the Julia/Simca book and ran with it, and as it turned out the book gave Alfred A. Knopf the Company plenty of cause to celebrate although it was years before Alfred A. Knopf the Man would acknowledge he had a masterpiece on his hands.

And that is how the first volume of *Mastering the Art of French Cooking* made it into print. It took ten years and two very determined women to write it and another woman, just as determined, who loved good food as much as she loved good books, to act as midwife and preside over its birth.

Oh yes, there was another author, Louisette Bertholle, way at the beginning. Some say it was her idea to write the book in the first place. The real story is that a woman named Lucille Tyree in Grosse Pointe, Michigan, told Louisette, who was visiting there and had made a *boeuf mode*, how much she loved French cooking and that what the United States really needed after the dreary food of the 1940's was a French cookbook specifically for Americans; Louisette went home to France and told Simca, who then met Julia, and how *they* met is another story altogether. After her initial contribution, Louisette married a French count and moved to the country. And

Mastering—as its disciples refer to it—went on to acquire the luster of legend. After thirty years in print it seems likely to live forever. For it is not just a cookbook. It is also a record of a way of life that was sweet in France.

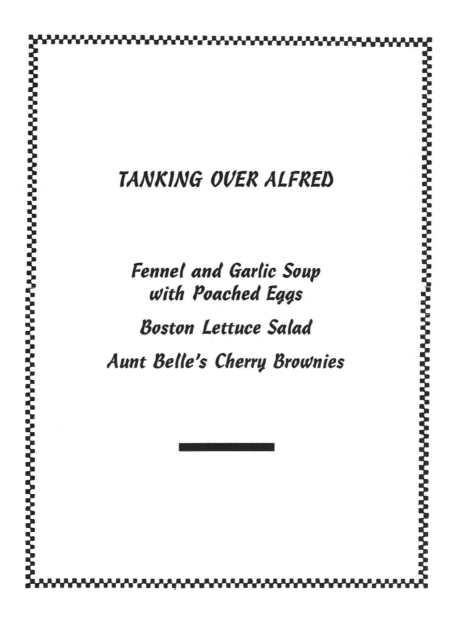

TANKING OVER ALFRED

Fennel and Garlic Soup with Poached Eggs

Boston Lettuce Salad

Aunt Belle's Cherry Brownies

Imagining Julia and her new pal Avis confronting an empty fridge, then foraging in Avis's son's vegetable patch for reinforcements, I have conjured up this main course vegetable soup with poached eggs. Made with fennel and garlic, tomatoes and olive oil, it has a Mediterranean feel to it and, although filling, has light clear tastes due in part to the vegetable, not meat-based, stock. The eggs, apart from making the soup more nourishing, also add a special texture when the slightly runny yolk breaks and combines with the broth. Bulb fennel is available during most months now, but if it is not, a combination of other vegetables could be used—celery and green beans, for instance—although the delicate anise fragrance of the fennel, so good with garlic, would be missing. Fresh basil, added at the last minute, gives that special green pungence to the soup that is the essence of sunny flavors (cooked basil can never do this; its flavor and color just fade away). This recipe is my instinctive version of how I think Julia would have done it, and, having known and admired her and her work for as many years as I have, I think I've gotten it right. The garlic taste in this dish, incidentally, is soft, as the garlic cooks a good while. Strong garlic can ruin a dish, unless the flavors surrounding it are just as strong; for me, generally, that means harsh food.

While Julia was perhaps simmering up a tasty soup that day in Cambridge, no doubt Avis was concocting dessert. Her best brownies—Aunt Belle's cherry brownies—were surely it. Simple enough to end an earthy dinner, these brownies have the coolness of juicy cherries running through them. The original recipe called for candied cherries, which, if you lived in northern Michigan and made your own as Avis's Aunt Belle did, would no doubt have been delicious. But commercially made candied cherries are pretty gruesome, and fresh cherries—or fresh raspberries or even olallieberries—are grand with chocolate and give the brownies extra moistness.

FENNEL AND GARLIC SOUP
WITH POACHED EGGS

∎∎

Serves 8

10 tablespoons olive oil
1 medium onion, peeled and sliced
1 large shallot, peeled and sliced
8 garlic cloves, sliced
2 carrots, peeled and thinly sliced
*1¼ pounds bulb fennel, trimmed of its ferns and any bruised
    bits, rinsed and thinly sliced*
Salt and freshly ground pepper to taste
¼ cup raw white rice
½ pound ripe plum tomatoes, sliced
1 pound zucchini, trimmed, rinsed and thinly sliced
8 eggs (freshest possible)
Vinegar
12 ¼-inch slices French bread, cut in half
1 cup grated good Parmesan cheese
8 large basil leaves, torn into small pieces

Heat 4 tablespoons of the olive oil in a large pot set over medium-low heat. Add the onion, shallot and garlic, stir briefly to coat with the oil, cover and cook gently for 10 to 15 minutes, stirring frequently. Add the carrots and fennel, and stir to combine. Cover again and stew the aromatic ingredients for about 10 minutes, stirring occasionally. Uncover the pot and add 2 quarts water. Salt and pepper lightly and bring to the boil. Add the rice and cook at a gentle simmer for 15 minutes, stirring and scraping the bottom of the pot frequently. Add the tomatoes and zucchini and boil the soup for 5 minutes or so. Correct the seasoning with salt and pepper. Set aside until ready to serve.

Poach the eggs, three or four at a time, in a saucepan or skillet about two-thirds filled with lightly acidulated barely simmering water. Any vinegar in the ratio of 1 tablespoon to 1 quart of water works well for this. (Don't salt the water, as this will cause the egg whites to disperse, whereas vinegar helps hold the eggs together.) To poach the eggs, simply crack them, one at a time, into the water, then gently spoon the white around the yolk until the egg more or less holds its shape. Sometimes it is helpful to crack the egg into a small Pyrex custard cup and slip it down the side of the pan for 10 to 15 seconds until the egg has begun to cook, then release it into the simmering water and spoon the white around the yolk as described above. After 1½ to 2 minutes, depending on how you like your eggs (the yolks should remain slightly runny), lift the eggs out of the water using a slotted spoon and lay them on a large plate lined with a kitchen towel or 2 or 3 thicknesses of paper towel to drain. When they are cool, trim the eggs with scissors to tidy them up if you wish. Set aside until ready to use.

Preheat the oven to 300° F.

Lay the slices of French bread on a baking sheet and bake them for 10 to 15 minutes to dry out; turn the slices once or twice as they crisp up. Brush generously with some of the olive oil, sprinkle with some of the Parmesan cheese and run the croûtons under a very hot broiler for 30 to 40 seconds, until lightly browned and the cheese is melted.

Place the poached eggs in warmed soup plates, divide the basil leaves among the dishes, then ladle the very hot soup into the plates. Place 1 or 2 croûtons in each bowl, spoon a bit of the remaining olive oil over them, sprinkle with some of the cheese and grind some black pepper over all. Serve with additional olive oil and cheese on the side.

A simple green salad would be good served either before or after this substantial soup.

Note: Tips on Poached Eggs

The freshest eggs tend to hold together best for poaching.

Poached eggs don't really need to be refrigerated unless you have made them several hours in advance, in which case be sure to take the chill off them by dropping them into hot water for a few moments, then allowing them to dry again on a towel before proceeding with the recipe. In recipes that require a very handsome poached egg, it is customary to float the eggs in water until they are served, which prevents them from flattening out; however, in this dish they are hidden by the soup and their appearance is less important.

AUNT BELLE'S CHERRY BROWNIES

A 9-inch square pan for 8 to 10

1 cup unbleached all-purpose flour
1¾ cups sugar
½ teaspoon salt
4 ounces unsweetened chocolate
1½ sticks unsalted butter
4 eggs
¼ cup milk
2 teaspoons vanilla extract
1 cup roughly chopped walnuts
1 cup pitted fresh sweet (Bing) cherries, roughly chopped

Preheat the oven to 300° F.

Stir together the dry ingredients in a large mixing bowl. In a heavy-bottomed saucepan melt the chocolate and butter together over low heat, stirring occasionally. Lightly beat the eggs with the milk and vanilla and add to the flour mixture along with the melted chocolate and butter mixture. Stir until smooth. Stir in the walnuts and cherries along with any accumulated cherry juice. Pour into a greased 9-inch square baking pan and bake for about 1 hour and 5 to 10 minutes; a toothpick inserted into the brownies should come out not dry but with a faint, sticky, not wet, coating. Cool on a rack, then cut into squares and serve plain or with vanilla ice cream or barely sweetened lightly beaten cream.

Note: Brownies will actually improve in flavor and texture after a day or two.

4

··

THE WOMAN
WHO LOVED
SHE-CRAB SOUP
AND THE
PRINCE
OF WALES

Baltimore, Maryland

Wally Warfield was pretty much the unsinkable type. Growing up poor in her mother's boarding house on drab Biddle Street didn't stop her from appearing at the age of ten on the society page of the *Baltimore Sun*, riding her pony. The other branches of the Wallis and Warfield clans were prosperous, and so was her Aunt Bess Merryman, who made sure the small, dark little girl of poor relations had plenty of advantages. Wally was later enrolled at one of the outposts of Maryland gentility, Oldfields Girl's School, and by the time she was seventeen all the accessories of mainline Baltimore respectability clung to her. Many young Baltimore debutantes, ripe for plucking, would have settled back and waited for a prince to come calling. Not Wally. The hardship of growing up poor among rich relations had taught her personal industry; and in learning the conformity of Baltimore society she also learned to shrug it off.

Those shrugs were not exactly unknown in the Wallis Warfield genes. John Merryman, one of Wally's ancestors and the proprietor of one of the famous Maryland estates, Hayfields, was a supporter of the South in an ostensibly Northern state during the Civil War. He sent money and supplies to the Confederate Army and for his trouble was imprisoned at Fort McHenry by the Feds. Later on, another branch of the Wallace family, though rural swells, often didn't behave as such and drove around in pickups and used four-

51

letter words. Wally's own defiance of local customs became evident in her rumored romantic escapades, which she followed by two marriages before abandoning American men altogether. And why wouldn't she? Any Baltimore woman who loved she-crab soup, that delicacy of the South—South Carolina, to be exact—and not the rough peppery red crab soups of her hometown, obviously had roving tastes. Most women could have found plenty of distinction in the eminent goods of Baltimore and not have looked farther.

Wallis Warfield looked farther, and in marrying the King she gave up the King. She loved the man.

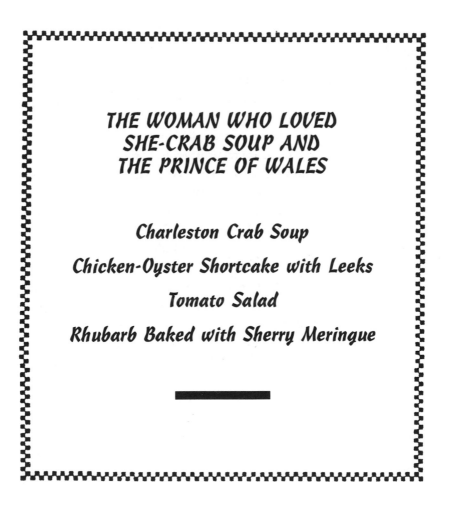

THE WOMAN WHO LOVED SHE-CRAB SOUP AND THE PRINCE OF WALES

Charleston Crab Soup

Chicken-Oyster Shortcake with Leeks

Tomato Salad

Rhubarb Baked with Sherry Meringue

In 1942 the Duchess of Windsor published a book of her favorite recipes. In the introduction the Duchess writes: "I myself am most familiar, of course, with southern cooking. I have been very happy to help carry some of the well-known dishes of my native land to other countries, and especially to have served on my table southern dishes which appeal to the Duke. It is the simple dishes of my homeland which are most popular to me, and which are the ones most frequently served at my table." The page is signed Wallis Windsor.

Those simple dishes include, not surprisingly, a recipe for Charleston Crab Soup, that delicate creamy concoction of the South that is especially sweet, it is said, when made with she-crabs. Of course it can be made with he-crabs too, and in either case, a small dose of a good, late-harvest-type dessert wine that simmers in the crab broth will give the soup a faint golden flavor. It is very important not to salt the soup until you have finished making it, since the crabs lend savor of their own as the dish progresses. This is the kind of crab dish that (if possible) should be made with fresh live crabs even though it may seem messy and laborious to do so. Because the soup is delicate and contains no robust flavors, the quality of the crab meat, and especially the crab-flavored broth, is crucial. Taste it, and you will understand why this native Baltimore woman loved it so well. (The recipe is written with procedures for both the daintier blue crabs of the East and the big bruiser Dungeness crabs of the West.)

The pairing of fowl with shellfish occurs in French cooking in the famous dish *poulet aux écrevisses* (chicken with crayfish), and one imagines that at luncheons around the Chesapeake Bay during the earlier part of the century, a brinier version of that dish—a chicken shortcake with oysters—was quite popular too. The Duchess of Windsor made it quite rich; I have taken it and made it not too rich at all, and have added leeks for color and flavor. There was a lot of beige cooking in those days: based in butterfat and bland to look at. The shortcake in this dish, by the way, is really a kind of cornbread, made interesting by the addition of a small amount of buckwheat flour.

The rhubarb dessert is just what you want after the rich flavors of crabs and oysters and the strength of stock-based sauces. It is plain, light, tart and not beige.

CHARLESTON CRAB SOUP

Serves 6

5 tablespoons butter
1 medium leek, root end and any torn green leaves trimmed, thoroughly washed and coarsely chopped
2 carrots, scrubbed, peeled and chopped
2 stalks celery, washed and chopped
4 pounds Chesapeake Bay blue crabs boiled, picked, with meat, shells, and butter reserved*
1 tomato, rinsed and coarsely chopped
1 cup good-quality dessert wine—a Sauternes or late-harvest Johannisberg Riesling
1 branch of fresh thyme, or 1 teaspoon dried thyme leaves
Small bunch of parsley (preferably flat-leaf parsley), chopped
2 cups milk
¼ cup heavy cream
2 egg yolks
Salt and freshly ground pepper to taste
Drops of fresh lemon juice
2 teaspoons finely chopped fresh tarragon (optional)

Melt the butter in a large pot, add the leek, carrots and celery, cover and allow to stew gently for 10 minutes, stirring frequently. Uncover the pot, add the crab shells along with any reserved liquid and the chopped tomato. Stir the crab shells into the aromatic vegetables until they are well distributed. Add the wine and simmer for 2 to 3 minutes, then add enough water (about 2 quarts) to barely cover, the thyme and parsley and simmer for 30 to 40 minutes, stirring occasionally. Strain through a very fine sieve. You should have about 1½ quarts crab stock. (If you have more, simply boil it down.)

Place the crab stock in a large saucepan and add the milk. Stir together the cream and egg yolks. Whisk a small amount of the hot crab stock into the cream and egg yolk mixture, then whisk the enrichment back into the stock. Stir steadily over medium-low heat until the soup nears a simmer and thickens *very* slightly. Don't let the soup boil; however, if the soup does overheat and the yolks scramble, whip it in the blender to smooth it out again. Correct the seasoning with salt and pepper and add lemon juice to taste. Stir in the tarragon, if desired.

To serve, place a small amount of crab meat and crab butter in the bottom of warmed soup plates. Ladle in the hot soup and serve.

*Note: This crab soup can also be made successfully with West Coast Dungeness crab. Use 4 pounds live crabs and drop them into lightly salted boiling water for 6 to 10 minutes, depending on their size. Drain, and when cool use the blunt edge of a cleaver to crack the claws and legs. Remove all the meat from the crabs, reserving any crab butter and all the shells, and discarding the gills. Proceed with the recipe as directed.

I do not give detailed instructions for dissecting and removing the meat from freshly cooked crabs. If you are unfamiliar with this procedure, an excellent description with diagrams can be found in *Mastering the Art of French Cooking* Volume II.

CHICKEN-OYSTER SHORTCAKE
WITH LEEKS

••

Serves 6

The Shortcake

½ cup unbleached all-purpose flour
¼ cup buckwheat flour
½ cup cornmeal
1½ teaspoons baking powder
1½ teaspoons sugar
½ teaspoon salt
1 egg, lightly beaten
⅔ cup milk
2 tablespoons butter, melted

Chicken-Oyster Filling

2 large chicken breasts
3 cups good chicken broth, lightly seasoned
2½ tablespoons butter
3 tablespoons flour
1 small leek, trimmed, thoroughly washed and finely chopped
    (to make about 1 cup)
1 tablespoon heavy cream
Salt and freshly ground pepper to taste
8 to 10 freshly shucked oysters with their liquor
1 teaspoon chopped fresh thyme leaves, or ½ teaspoon dried
    thyme leaves
Juice of ½ lemon (more if needed)

Preheat the oven to 400° F.

Prepare the shortcake: Sift together the dry ingredients. Combine the egg and milk and add to the dry mixture along with the melted butter, stirring until well blended. Pour into a buttered 8-inch round or square pan and bake for 20 to 25 minutes, until the shortcake is lightly browned. Cool in the pan for 15 to 20 minutes, then run a knife around the edge and invert onto an ovenproof plate or platter. Cover with foil to keep warm.

Prepare the filling: Poach the chicken breasts at a slow simmer in the chicken broth for about 15 minutes (they should remain slightly pink at the bone as the meat will finish cooking when it reheats in the sauce). Place the chicken on a plate to cool; pour the broth into a Pyrex measure and spoon away the fat that accumulates on the surface.

Melt the butter in a large heavy-bottomed saucepan. Stir in the flour and cook the *roux* over low heat for 2 to 3 minutes, stirring frequently. Add the chicken broth all at once and whisk continuously over medium heat until the sauce boils and thickens. Add the leek, lower the heat and gently cook the sauce for about 5 minutes, until the leek is just tender. Add the cream; set aside. (The sauce may wait at this point for an hour or two at room temperature, with a piece of plastic wrap pressed directly onto its surface.)

When the chicken is cool enough to handle remove the skin and bones and, using your fingers, pull apart the meat into bite-size pieces (you can chop the chicken with a knife but this gives the dish a processed look). Season the chicken lightly with salt and pepper. If the oysters are large, slice them in half or even into quarters.

Rewarm the shortcake in the oven if it has cooled. Rewarm the sauce gently, add the chicken, the oysters and oyster liquor, and stir over medium heat for a minute or two to rewarm the chicken and gently poach the oysters. Correct the seasoning with salt and pepper; stir in the thyme and lemon juice to taste.

Slice the shortcake into wedges or squares, split each slice through the middle and place on individual plates. Spoon the hot chicken-oyster mixture between the pieces and on top of the shortcake.

RHUBARB BAKED WITH SHERRY MERINGUE

••

Serves 6

2 pounds tender spring rhubarb, trimmed, washed and cut
    into ½-inch pieces (peel mature rhubarb, which tends to
    be slightly stringy)
¾ cup sugar
½ cup honey
4 egg whites at room temperature
¼ teaspoon salt
¼ teaspoon cream of tartar
2 tablespoons good dry sherry
Powdered sugar in a shaker

Preheat the oven to 350° F.

Place the rhubarb in a 6-cup buttered shallow baking dish, add
¼ cup of the sugar and the honey, cover with a piece of foil and
bake until the rhubarb is tender, about 30 to 35 minutes. (If the
cooked rhubarb is too tart, add a little more sugar or honey.) Beat
the egg whites with the salt and cream of tartar until they form soft
peaks, then gradually add the remaining ½ cup sugar, beating until
the whites are almost stiff. Stir in the sherry and spread over the
rhubarb. Return to the oven for 6 to 8 minutes, until the meringue
is slightly browned. Dust with the powdered sugar and spoon onto
plates.

5

PATSY'S MOM

Winchester, Virginia

I f you're looking for Winchester, Virginia, just look for apples because that's what grows there most. Sturdy apple trees surround the modest town and fill a spacious deep-green valley. In late summer when the apples weigh down old branches and the first crop is picked, the canning places around town put on extra shifts and working mothers come home late.

For years, in the thirties and forties, that's what Patsy's mom did. Of course, back then she was Ginny's mom. No one on bumpy South Kent Street had ever heard of Patsy Cline the singing star in those days. The girl named Virginia—Ginny for short—was just the eldest of three Hensley children, helping her mother keep the family safe and holding her young dreams inside.

It wasn't so much that times were tough in Shenandoah Valley towns before and after the War. It was just that it took a lot of work to keep life going. Ginny's dad, when he was there, had trouble providing for his family. So even with extra shifts at the cannery, Mom Hensley often worked at home as a seamstress, sometimes assisted by Ginny. On a sweltering day in July or August though, Ginny would peer out the back door of the small wooden house, slither down the slope of withering grass to where the maple shade was thick, and it would take an extra holler to remind her of the pile of hemming that didn't care if it was hot or not. Whenever her mom needed her, Ginny usually was there. She'd been born when her mom was sixteen and, more like a sister to her than a daughter, Ginny helped her mom raise the other children with few grumbles.

By 1950 Hilda Hensley could see that she had more than just an industrious seventeen-year-old on her hands. She had, loud and clear, a seventeen-year-old with talent, not to mention daring. Taking the hills from Winchester High to Gaunt's Drugstore at a full run to pump sodas and scoop ice cream after school was one thing. Hitching a ride at night to perform at the Wagon Wheel on the West Virginia line was quite something else. People had known for some time that Ginny was clever. She could sit at the piano and play a tune pulled out of her head or off the radio, and get it right on the first try. But Ginny Hensley had something else that made people forget all that and stopped them dead in their tracks. She had a voice, the kind that you could never forget.

"Mom" Hensley knew that having a gifted daughter was just fine, but in the meantime there was food to be put on the table. Singing could have a place in the Hensley home, but it would have to follow the work of keeping a family alive and loved. The Hensley women, accustomed to working overtime, took this in stride. When Hilda drove Ginny to singing dates in their '47 Ford, the other kids went along; later on, when Ginny had her own children, often the babies would accompany Ginny and Hilda, who was still at the wheel. No one ever got rich off those early engagements, and no one ever complained. Hilda loved her gifted girl, and that kept her going.

Ginny's career never did make her mother rich, not even long after Ginny became Patsy—from her middle name Patterson—and added her first husband's name, Cline, to create the name the world would eventually know.

But when Patsy Cline's moment of glory came, it brought something more precious than wealth to Hilda Hensley: It brought her a mother's pride. Seeing Patsy radiant in Winchester's annual Apple Blossom Parade, coasting down Main Street in a black Cadillac convertible, gave a deep happiness to the woman who had struggled so long to make her children a respected part of a hometown that was wary of working-class folks. Stardom was all very well—Patsy craved it, and achieved it—but for Hilda, the town's eventual, if grudging, recognition gave as much substance to Patsy's success as any hit record. For the Hensley women, worth always began at home. As Patsy's stature grew, and love of her music graced her life but took her far away, Patsy sometimes lost that sense of home. But like her mother, Patsy possessed a tremendous good heart that would, Hilda knew, stand by her all her life.

Not that Patsy didn't run into trouble now and then. When she was twenty-nine and finally leading the life of a big singing star in Nashville, Patsy was nearly killed in a head-on car crash in the newly paved outskirts of the city. She owed her life to the nearby Seventh-Day Adventist Hospital but after eight weeks there, and an interminably strict vegetarian diet, Patsy was starved for something tasty. Sylvia, Patsy's sister, had smuggled in cheeseburgers and fries to the delight of a still very bruised but bored Patsy who was dying to be out of the damn bland hospital and doing what she was meant to be doing—singing and making hit records, loving her husband Charlie Dick and taking care of their babies. Patsy's face was black and blue, her ribs broken and her heart sore from missing home. So one night Hilda came to the rescue with fried chicken salad with boiled dressing and homemade ham biscuits. Patsy tucked in that night, with all the great appetite she had for good food and life itself. In between bites, with her spirits on the rise, her warm deep laugh floated down the halls of the hushed-up hospital, giving it for at least one night that glorious Patsy Cline sound. Hilda, perched on the bed and enjoying some of her own good cooking, smiled at her daughter's full appetite and added her own gentle laugh to the early spring evening.

That was all twenty-seven years ago. Patsy recovered from that terrible accident and went on to sing in the last months of her life some of her most powerful songs. "Crazy," which many consider her greatest, was recorded with Patsy's ribs still giving her pain. A year later she was dead, killed at the age of thirty in a plane crash in some forsaken forest between Dyersburg and Nashville. A mother's joy became, from one day to the next, a mother's grief. Today, for Hilda, who is now seventy-three, the grief is somewhat less, replaced by remembrance. In the white-board Hensley house, still on worn-looking South Kent Street, but across from the empty house of Patsy's childhood, memories of Patsy are plentiful. The most striking one is a portrait of a richly smiling, expectant Patsy that sits near the still-working sewing machine by the front window. Mild valley light settles on the photograph where Patsy wrote, "To Mom—we finally made it. All my love."

Remembrance of some sort always follows a loss. But if you are born to sing and sing greatly—and had a mother to help get you there—then you are also born to be remembered deeply.

Patsy is. Just ask her mom.

PATSY'S MOM

Fried Chicken Salad with Mustard Greens and Boiled Dill Dressing

Cream Biscuits with Virginia Ham

Shenandoah Valley Apple Gingerbread

Fried chicken in one form or another seems always present in a Virginia kitchen. About-to-be-fried, just-fried, or day-old fried, it's always there to fill in the gaps. Putting fried chicken, with its rough dry skin, in a salad with smooth Romaine leaves, tangy mustard greens and a warm boiled dressing is a good way to make leftover chicken ready for company again. It is about the best cold poultry salad you could ever want. If a nonsweet dressing is preferred, any homemade salad dressing with herbs would be good.

There are lots of biscuit recipes around, but making them with cream instead of milk and adding a little vegetable shortening with the butter makes them tender and flaky beyond belief.

I have loved gingerbread since I was a boy, and when I stumbled onto Virginia-style gingerbread, I was hooked. It is chewy rather than cakey, and sweetened only with molasses, it is not oversweet. This kind of gingerbread makes a fine upside-down dessert with flavorful autumn apples and a squirt of bourbon to give it that close-to-Tennessee taste.

FRIED CHICKEN SALAD
WITH MUSTARD GREENS
AND BOILED DILL DRESSING

This salad is just as good made with leftover fried chicken; besides the Boiled Dill Dressing, any salad dressing with herbs would be good.

If you wish, the chicken can be browned in the hot oil until it has a nice crust (about 10 minutes), then placed in an ovenproof dish and baked in a 425° F. oven for 15 to 20 minutes. The skin will be as crisp but the chicken will have absorbed less oil.

Serves 4

Vegetable shortening or oil for frying
Salt and freshly ground pepper to taste
1 3½- to 4-pound fresh chicken, cut up
½ cup flour
1 teaspoon salt
10 to 12 Romaine lettuce leaves and curly mustard greens,
 washed and dried, the larger leaves torn into 2 or 3 pieces
1¾ cups Boiled Dill Dressing, still warm (recipe follows)
2 or 3 radishes, washed, trimmed and cut into slivers

Place a large heavy skillet over medium heat and add the shortening or oil (there should be about ⅛ inch of fat in the pan for frying). While the pan is heating, salt and pepper both sides of the chicken pieces. Mix together the flour, the 1 teaspoon salt and some fresh pepper. Toss the chicken in the flour mixture until all the pieces are evenly coated.

When the oil is hot (a piece of chicken should begin to sizzle gently when placed in the pan), add the chicken and fry it for 20 to 25 minutes, depending on the size of the pieces and the actual temperature of the oil. Turn the chicken several times as it cooks; for very juicy white meat, remove the breasts 3 or 4 minutes before the dark meat. The chicken should be a medium golden brown when it is done (if you cook it too quickly it will be too dark). Remove the chicken from the pan to cool, pressing each piece with a pair of tongs and shaking it briefly over the skillet to remove any remaining oil. Pour off the fat from the pan, reserving ¼ cup of the browned pan drippings at the bottom to use in the boiled dressing (recipe follows).

When the chicken has cooled, pull the skin and meat off the bones and shred it into more or less bite-size morsels (do this with your fingers). Place the chicken in a large bowl with the lettuce leaves and mustard greens, add ½ cup of the warm dressing and toss to coat the ingredients evenly. Correct the seasoning with salt and pepper. Arrange the salad on a platter or on individual plates, and sprinkle with the slivered radishes. Serve with the remaining dressing passed on the side.

BOILED DILL DRESSING

About 1¾ cups dressing

1 tablespoon corn oil
1 tablespoon flour
¼ cup pan drippings, from frying the chicken
1 cup milk
½ teaspoon dry mustard powder
2 teaspoons honey
1 teaspoon wine vinegar
Salt and freshly ground pepper to taste
Pinch of cayenne to taste
1 to 2 tablespoons lemon juice, to taste
2 tablespoons finely chopped fresh dill, or 1 teaspoon dried dill
1 tablespoon sour cream
¼ cup buttermilk

Heat the oil over medium heat in a heavy-bottomed saucepan, stir in the flour and cook it for 1 to 2 minutes. Add the reserved pan drippings, stir in the milk and whisk the dressing until it comes to the boil and has thickened slightly. Stir in the mustard, honey, vinegar, seasonings and lemon juice. Remove from the heat and allow to cool to lukewarm. Add the dill, sour cream and buttermilk as needed to obtain a good consistency (the dressing should not be too thick). If made in advance, set aside or refrigerate, then reheat gently just before using. The dressing is best served warm with the fried chicken salad, but for other uses it is also delicious cold—with leftover roast pork, for instance, or in place of the coleslaw dressing on page 233.

CREAM BISCUITS WITH VIRGINIA HAM

About 12 to 15 biscuits

2 cups unbleached all-purpose flour
1 tablespoon baking powder
½ teaspoon salt
2 to 3 tablespoons finely chopped Virginia ham
4 tablespoons cold unsalted butter, cut into small pieces
1 tablespoon solid vegetable shortening
1 cup heavy cream

Preheat the oven to 400° F.

Stir together the flour, baking powder, salt and ham. Blend in the butter and shortening, using the tips of your fingers (don't work for a perfect blend, the flour mixture should be rough). Using a fork, stir in the cream and work the dough until it begins to mass together. Press the dough into a ball, adding extra drops of cream to gather up any remaining dry bits. Roll the dough out on a lightly floured surface to an approximate 8-inch square; it should be about

¾ inch thick. Square the edges with a knife, then cut the dough into square biscuits any size you wish. Place on an ungreased baking sheet and bake for 10 to 12 minutes; the top of the biscuits should be a light golden brown (do not overbake or the baking powder tends to turn bitter). Serve hot or warm with soft butter.

Note: Unbaked biscuits freeze very successfully, and can be placed frozen into the oven (they will require an extra 2 or 3 minutes baking time).

SHENANDOAH VALLEY APPLE GINGERBREAD

A 12-inch dessert for 8 to 10

5 tablespoons butter
2 pounds tart green apples, peeled, cored and thinly sliced
¼ cup sugar
¼ cup bourbon
2 cups flour
1 teaspoon baking soda
1 teaspoon baking powder
½ teaspoon ground cloves
1 tablespoon ground ginger
1 teaspoon cinnamon
½ teaspoon salt
1 stick unsalted butter
1 cup boiling water
1½ cups molasses
2 eggs
Powdered sugar in a shaker or fine sieve

Melt the butter over medium-high heat in a 12-inch seasoned cast-iron skillet or a nonstick skillet with an ovenproof handle. Add the apples and cook them for 10 to 15 minutes, stirring and tossing them often. When the apples are tender, add the sugar and stir the apples slowly as they begin to caramelize. Pour in the bourbon and shake the pan while the alcohol evaporates. Set the apples aside in the skillet.

In a mixing bowl stir together the flour, baking soda, baking powder, spices and salt. Place the butter and hot water in another bowl and allow to stand until the butter has melted. Stir in the molasses, then beat in the eggs. Add the liquid ingredients to the flour mixture and beat until the batter is smooth.

Preheat the oven to 400° F.

Spread the apples over the bottom of the skillet into a smooth layer. Oil the sides of the skillet. Pour in the gingerbread batter and bake for 30 to 35 minutes, or until a knife inserted in the center comes out clean. Cool on a rack for 10 minutes, then invert onto a serving dish; if any of the apples stick to the skillet, just scrape them off with a spatula and spread them over the gingerbread. While the dessert is still warm, sprinkle a few drops of bourbon over the apples, dust the edges with powdered sugar, cut into wedges and serve. Plain unbeaten or lightly beaten cream may accompany the gingerbread.

6

OH JOHN

Charlottesville, Virginia

The dining table at Oakencroft Farm—the 250-acre Rogan estate near Charlottesville, Virginia—may not have been dark and forbidding like the one at Grandmother Munnie's house, but to Rosemary Rogan's eternal disgust, it was just as long. Sitting at her family's table in the early 1950's with her brother, two sisters and parents, Rosemary often felt the sting not just of her mother's iced-tea spoon rapping Rosemary's elbow when it strayed too close to the uncouth zone of Table's Edge, but also of brute wealth strangling her search for beauty. In the Rogan house, breeding was everything. And although a Rogan, Rosemary was born caring for Beethoven, not breeding.

The only place eight-year-old Rosy was really happy was in the kitchen. It was where the love was. Cassie and Robert, the black couple who worked for the Rogans, didn't care if Rosemary was fat and didn't look good in white tennis outfits and listened to Beethoven and Bach instead of the Mills Brothers like everyone else in the house did. They didn't sigh and say "Oh John" all the time like Rosemary's mother did to her father. Rosemary's mother said "Oh John" until Rosemary felt like screaming. "Oh John" look at Rosemary's curtsy when she passes the hors-d'oeuvre. "Oh John" why does she spend more time with the help than with us. "Oh John" how can Rosy be a debutante (what she was trying to say but found

73

too indelicate to utter was, "Oh John, how can we have a FAT debutante?!"). In the kitchen there was no "Oh John," just love and heavenly fragrant disorder, and a *round* table where the kids could sit together on their parents' night out to eat their supper of well-done hamburger and mashed potatoes, and toss peas at each other or flip prune whip onto the beige walls.

Apart from Cassie and Robert, Rosemary's other pal in the house was Fannie the babysitter, who was big and loud. On the nights that Mama and Papa Rogan dined out, the pedigreed hush behind the brick walls and soaring white columns of the Rogan house reeled under Fannie's robust flourishes. She wore Mary Poppins shoes and reassured Rosemary that if a burglar came (and Rosemary fretted about burglars) Fannie would take care of him by hollering down the stairs, "Honey, just wait a minute 'til I get my bathrobe on and I'll be right down." Fannie livened things up and didn't frown when Rosemary carted food up to her bedroom, which, besides the kitchen, was the only place she enjoyed eating. In her bedroom, away from her parents' stares of disappointment, Rosemary could munch unobserved on her favorite things, like crackers and dry cereal (she could polish off a whole box of Cheerios in one session with Fannie) and peppermint ice cream.

One of Rosy's most gleeful childhood memories was the evening she and Fannie were perched on the pink organdy princess beds in her room devouring big bowls of chocolate ice cream when suddenly they heard footsteps on the front porch. These were not burglar's footsteps; much worse, they were Mama and Papa Rogan's. Caught in the act of two cardinal sins—eating in the bedroom and *entertaining the help* in the bedroom—Rosemary the Swift knew just what to do. She snatched up several layers of pink organdy and waved Fannie, clutching the two bowls of half-eaten ice cream, under the bed where she remained, choking with laughter, while the Rogans appeared to say goodnight. Rosemary finally got rid of her parents and dragged Fannie and the two bowls out from under the bed and the two friends, with guffaws in between mouthfuls, polished off their ice cream.

Rosemary Rogan basically grew up a loner, and until she left home for boarding school at the age of fifteen she found solace in a private Rosemary World inhabited by loving black cooks and butlers and a heroic man named Ludwig van, and by her piano and her six-string folk guitar, which she liked to strum late at night, sitting near her bedroom window and looking out at the cows on the hills of middle Virginia. Rosemary also found relief from the lonely Rogan landscape at her grandmother Oh Maw's house near Charlottesville.

The Rogan kids always had their birthdays at Oh Maw's (a very young Rosemary once heard her grandfather exclaim "Oh Boy" as he read the newspaper and she decided to call her maternal grandparents Oh Boy and Oh Maw). Sure, there was ceremony at Westmere, Oh Maw's spread. But unlike at Oakencraft it was *shared* ceremony. Oh Maw liked to cook and was involved in the kitchen with her cook, Rebecca. The two of them produced the best food Rosemary ever ate, wonderful meals cooked not for show but from love of good food. One of Rosemary's favorites was a pork roast that cooked with cabbage and white wine and cream until it all sort of melted together. Rosy also lived off the airy dinner rolls that she stuffed full of Virginia ham and crammed into her pockets before skipping out the back door—probably more accurately described as the rear entrance—into the sunny blur of Oh Maw's beautiful gardens. Oh Maw loved flowers and could make gardenias thrive even through Virginia frosts. Her trick with the gardenias when a frost warning was issued was to have the immense urns containing them put into the heated garages for safety at night. But one year a plane flew low during a frost and triggered the garage door devices at Westmere. The next morning Rosemary, making her early rounds, found Oh Maw and her gardeners standing by the gaping garage doors and surveying the gardenia carnage inside. But then it was time for breakfast so no one dwelt overlong on the scene and Oh Maw, after making arrangements for the next generation of gardenias, took Rosy by the hand and walked her out of the chill into the warm kitchen.

OH JOHN

Rebecca's Succotash Soup
Pork Braised with Cabbage and Cream
Applesauce with Brown Sugar and Rum
Boiled or Steamed Rice
Cracker Pie

Rosy loved the food at Oh Maw's because for the most part it was more for eating than for admiring (although dinners at West-mere were always handsomely presented). Rebecca's succotash soup was one of Westmere's specialties, a simple variation of what is usually a vegetable dish. The pork roast braised with cabbage and accompanied by homemade rum-flavored applesauce is exactly the kind of dish, gently flavored and rather rich, that you would find at a dressy Virginia dinner. Cracker pie, sometimes called mock apple pie, is actually a kind of meringue. Although often made with walnuts, cracker pie in Oh Maw's house was made with pecans since the recipe came from a cousin who owned a pecan farm over in Alabama. Whipped cream flavored with sherry, served on the side, gives a delicate nudge to the cracker pie and tames its sweetness somewhat.

While a pork loin roast can be used in the following recipe, pork shoulder always gives a moister and more flavorful result when given a long cooking. For the crackers in the pie, use simple soda crackers, or cream crackers, preferably without salt. Uneeda (as in "you need a . . .!") biscuits were once ideal to use but are now distributed by Nabisco mostly just in the East.

REBECCA'S SUCCOTASH SOUP

(Note: I have left this recipe substantially in the words of Rebecca, Oh Maw's cook at Westmere.)

Serves 6 to 8

1 piece of salt pork the size of an egg
3 cups fresh large forkhood lima beans
3 cups uncooked fresh corn cut off the cob (about 4 or 5 ears)
4 tablespoons butter
1 cup rich milk (or cream)
1 tablespoon sugar
Salt and freshly ground pepper to taste

Put the salt pork on to boil in a quart of water and let it get tender (30 to 40 minutes of simmering). Add the lima beans and cook 5 or 6 minutes, until the beans are just tender. Add the corn (fresh ingredients are the best) and let cook 4 or 5 minutes more. Add the butter, milk, sugar, and season to taste with salt and pepper. Serve in low bowls.

PORK BRAISED WITH CABBAGE AND CREAM

Serves 6 to 8

3 pounds green cabbage (about 1½ heads)
3 tablespoons butter
½ cup chopped onions
1 garlic clove, peeled and minced
½ teaspoon salt
Freshly ground pepper to taste
1 3½- to 4-pound loin or shoulder pork roast at room
*   temperature, trimmed of all fat*
3 tablespoons oil
½ cup dry white wine
1 cup heavy cream
1 bay leaf
3 tablespoons grated good Parmesan cheese

Chop the cabbage and cook it in a large quantity of salted boiling water for 3 or 4 minutes; drain. Melt the butter in a large skillet and cook the onions and garlic over medium-low heat for 3 or 4 minutes. Add the cabbage, the ½ teaspoon salt, some fresh pepper, and cook and stir for 5 minutes or until the moisture has evaporated.

Preheat the oven to 350° F.

Pat the meat dry, and season it with salt and pepper. In a large pot heat the oil and in it sear the pork on all sides. Remove the pork from the pan, pour out the fat and pour in the white wine, scraping the bottom and sides of the pan to dissolve any caramelized meat juices. Return the meat to the pan with the cabbage. Pour the cream over all, add the bay leaf and bring to the simmer. Lay a piece of parchment paper or wax paper over the meat, cover with a lid and bake for 1½ hours, turning the meat once or twice as it braises. Uncover the pot, remove the paper, sprinkle the Parmesan cheese over the top and bake 30 minutes longer. Remove the meat, place it on a carving board, cover with a piece of foil and allow to rest for 20 minutes or so. Divide the pork into desired portions (it should be very tender, almost falling apart), season lightly with salt and pepper and arrange it on a platter. Correct the seasoning of the cabbage and cream sauce and spoon it over and around the meat. Serve with rice and the applesauce (recipe follows).

Note: The idea of placing a piece of parchment paper or wax paper over meat that is cooking in liquid is an old French braising technique to keep the meat moist. When steam hits a hot metal lid it evaporates, but when it hits paper it condenses and bastes the meat.

APPLESAUCE WITH BROWN SUGAR AND RUM

•••

Serves 6 to 8

8 large green apples (4 pounds), peeled and thinly sliced
½ teaspoon grated lemon zest
2 teaspoons lemon juice
½ cup brown sugar
3 tablespoons Jamaican rum
3 tablespoons butter

Place the apples and lemon zest in a large heavy-bottomed nonaluminum pot. Cover and stew the apples over low heat, stirring occasionally, for about 30 minutes. Uncover and beat the apples with a wooden spoon to make a rough applesauce. Stir in the lemon juice, brown sugar, rum and butter, and cook, uncovered, over medium heat, stirring, until thickened, for about 10 minutes. Serve warm or hot with the braised pork.

Note: Jamaican rum, readily available, has by far the best flavor, but other rums are okay in a pinch.

CRACKER PIE

....

A 9-inch dessert for 6 to 8

3 egg whites at room temperature
Pinch of salt
1½ teaspoons vanilla extract, or ¼ teaspoon almond extract
¾ cup sugar
9 unsalted or lightly salted soda crackers about 3 inches in
*   diameter, not too finely crushed*
1 teaspoon baking powder
1 cup broken pecans
Powdered sugar in a shaker

For the topping

1 cup heavy cream
2 tablespoons sugar
3 tablespoons dry sherry

Preheat the oven to 350° F.

Beat the egg whites with the salt until they form soft peaks. Add the extract, and gradually the sugar, beating until the whites are stiff. Add the crackers, the baking powder and the pecans and fold into the egg whites. Spoon into a well-buttered 9-inch pie plate, smooth evenly and bake for 25 minutes. Cool on a rack. Dust lightly with the powdered sugar.

To serve, cut wedges of the pie from the pan.

Pass the cream, lightly beaten with the sherry and sugar, on the side.

7

SLOW TIME

Walnut Flat, Kentucky

The kids of Walnut Flat, Kentucky, had a sure-fire system for aggravating the hell out of the school teacher. First, it had to be fall, around walnut season. And you couldn't use just any old walnuts, it had to be black walnuts that you knocked down with your dad into the bed of a pickup truck and took home and split the skin off by dumping them in your gravel driveway and driving back and forth over 'em. The final phase of the operation was pivotal, peeling off the skin and smashing open the nuts with a hammer and picking out the meat, all done in such a way as to achieve maximum exposure of two eight-year-old hands to the nasty indelible effects of black walnut stain. The rest was easy: spend the next three or four months—at least until January—being an eager-beaver hand-raiser in school, shooting up a grubby black paw at least twice at each available opportunity. The result was sheer magic.

There were other days of heaven along the Kentucky backroads, if it was the 1940's and you were a little red-haired kid named Sam. There were those summer afternoon departures, unannounced to your mom, on a bike pointed into town. Not that you couldn't be traced as you pedaled along Crab Orchard Road past the bluegrass rises and the four-board white fences that went on forever like a sideways railroad, containing the landscape and thwarting any possible sinister effect of the pretty sinister-looking black tobacco barns.

85

Those pristine fences secured the trip, and also marked the miles of yards and fields and houses from which the progress home of our idle bicycler was relayed by phone. Sam Matheny never strayed far from Elsferd Farm though, just far enough to make it seem sweet again.

Dairy farm life taught a kid a lot in those days. No, it wasn't only brat tactics useful at school, or the quiet evasions of the open road. Living separated by just two walls from forty head of dairy cattle, you also learned a lot about steadiness. Morning and night, twice a day, every day, those cows had to be milked. If you were assigned to milking, even when you were only eight, and one day you weren't there, there was immediate trouble. And immediate trouble was the kind you didn't want (delayed trouble was something else). Sam learned his first lesson about milking one day when he was two and trotted out to the barn with his dad. Before settling down to the milking, Ferdinand Matheny lifted his son onto a ledge where he could sit and watch, and set Sammy right on a long nail. The memory of that, and of his first tetanus shot, must have instilled in Sam the virtues of *doing* the milking over *not* doing the milking. He learned to be a steady milker and, in the process, learned the unceasing rhythms of country life. Those dawn or evening hours around the cows stilled your mind and, once done, you walked in calm to eat with the family.

The tastes of a dairy farm, too, were something you never forgot. You could always tell the farm kids at school because they wouldn't drink school milk: They couldn't stand the empty flavor of boiled milk. Kids like Sam grew up only knowing the gentle barny taste that curled through fresh Jersey milk. It's funny, though, while growing up around cows, leaning into their flanks day after day, squeezing, squeezing, and feeling warm trust in the squirts of milk—you never got close to a cow. Fond, maybe, but not close. Maybe that was because with a cow you were more like a partner than a friend. Sheep, though, were different from cows, or even pigs. A startling thing happened with sheep. They usually lambed in March on what always seemed like the coldest, most God-forsaken night of the year. Often the ewes ignored their young or even rejected them, and the only way to save the lambs was to cart them into the kitchen around the coal stove for a snuggle in your arms and a good warm bottle. That was the best, because lambs don't forget their first meal: Give them one heavenly, warm bottle and you are Mom for life.

Sam's Uncle Bob Matheny a few farms down the road knew about lambs better than anyone. Insulated by tobacco fields and occasional fields of broom corn from a world running foolishly on Fast Time, Sam's Uncle Bob lived—and still lives—his life as he has for eighty years, on nice sensible Slow Time. After the Second World War, when western Kentucky was wrenched out of central standard time, and rudely plunked down into eastern standard time, Bob Matheny took a stand—documented in newspapers coast to coast. The new time, which he called Fast Time, was a damn menace, and if his pigs and sheep couldn't tolerate it, neither could he, and he ignored it ever after. Bob Matheny always kept sheep, and he still has a flock of twenty-five roaming around. Hand-raised from birth, they are like family: sheared twice a year, then free again, nothing more menacing than shears ever gets near them. If you have to be a sheep, you're smart to check in at Uncle Bob's.

Looking back to Walnut Flat—where all that's left is the general store, recently shuttered after seventy years—Sam can't decide which times were best. He loved the fall, with its abrupt stillness after the harvest, when everyone took a breather and there was time to go gather walnuts, or just be together in the amber afternoons. But there were the spring days too, when Elsie Matheny packed a picnic of her famous pork salad with the first new onions, salt-risen rolls and maybe a black walnut pie. Those April picnics usually meant a drive up to Paris, Kentucky. There the family rented rowboats for two dollars a day and paddled up the nice deep mill-stream, shaded by arches of bigtooth maples, to the grassy bank of Clayborne Farms. The lunch was spread out and the Matheny bunch would feast, then loll in the blurry green of Kentucky spring, while the Clayborne horses would amble down the slopes and graze around the drowsy clan. It was hard to imagine they were the same beauties that blazed to glory and ribbons at the Keeneland trials and later at the Derby. All that didn't matter to Sammy though. To him those horses were just the quiet companions of spring.

September in 1990 is far removed from those days, but the recollections have come easy. On a Sunday afternoon, Sam Matheny is once again heading down Crab Orchard Road. He's got to check on some things at the farm. The neighbors aren't poking their heads out this time, tracking that truant bicycle, but they almost are, and Sam grins. Elsferd Farm—named for his mom and dad—is not home anymore, Los Angeles is. The family is long gone and the house is still. But the farm is still Sammy's, and as it comes closer he reaches deep into the sure days of Slow Time, and the present is suspended for a while. As we bump past some black walnut trees there is a whiff of mischief, and the buoyant days of a bluegrass boyhood appear again. After the farm we'll stop at Uncle Bob's. He's funny as a rubber crutch once he gets going.

SLOW TIME

Jellied Pork Salad with New Onions and Peas

Salt-rising Rolls

Caramelized Black Walnut Pie

Pork salad can be done all kinds of ways. You can cube leftover pork and stir it with mayonnaise, as you would other cold meat or poultry salads. Or you can go a noncreamy, more detailed route and cook the pork, and use the cooking flavorings and liquids specifically for a salad. The following pork salad is the latter kind: The meat simmers with aromatic vegetables, sliced lemon, herbs, some good stock (or just water) and a little vinegar. The liquid is then slightly jellied, with the addition of a small amount of gelatin (the pork jelly should be soft, not rubbery), and served with the reserved vegetables along with fresh peas and new onions. This is a delicate and refreshing spring salad and, once set, is easily packed for a picnic. The jelly for this dish is not clarified. It is not that kind of formal dish and also the jelly retains a fuller flavor when unfiltered. The jelly could also be made by adding pig's feet or knuckle to the pork as it braises, and eliminating the addition of powdered gelatin at the end. However, gelatin is generally more familiar and available than pig's feet, and the recipe is written accordingly.

Salt-rising rolls are fascinating. They are made with a starter of sliced potatoes, cornmeal and hot water stirred together and allowed to ferment slightly over a twenty-four-hour period. The essential thing is to use nondegerminated cornmeal, which is usually found at health food stores. The germ of the corn kernel, it seems, is essential for grabbing the wild yeasts and fueling the starter. Salt-rising dough got its name because it was originally put to rise in a bowl set in warmed rock salt, an excellent insulator. The dough, in fact, contains a relatively small amount of salt, but it does need to rise in a place warmer than conventional yeast doughs do; instructions are given for creating the right temperature. Salt-rising rolls (or bread, the dough makes either) has an individual fragrance, rather cheesey, but the taste is surprisingly mild. Marion Cunningham, who now writes the Fanny Farmer cookbooks, calls the taste "wholesome," which is exactly right.

It wouldn't be Walnut Flat, Kentucky, without black walnut pie. A lot of nut pies are made with corn syrup to give sweetness and texture, but this pie uses cream and sugar, which are reduced and caramelized, then reinforced with maple syrup, to achieve a deeper, finer flavor.

JELLIED PORK SALAD WITH NEW ONIONS AND PEAS

Serves 6

¼ cup olive oil
2 medium carrots, peeled and thinly sliced
3 stalks celery, thinly sliced
1 medium onion, peeled and sliced
Salt
1 4- to 5-pound pork shoulder roast (bone in), trimmed of most
    fat
1 lemon, rinsed and cut into round slices about ⅛ inch thick
3 garlic cloves, unpeeled
½ teaspoon whole black peppercorns
Several sprigs of parsley with stems
Sprigs of fresh thyme, or 1 teaspoon dried thyme leaves
1 bay leaf
2 tablespoons white wine vinegar
3 cups homemade chicken stock or water
Freshly ground pepper to taste
1 package unflavored gelatin, softened in 3 tablespoons cold
    water
2 pounds fresh peas, shelled
12 new onions or tiny leeks, rinsed, stems and tips of greens
    trimmed
Crisp lettuce leaves

Preheat the oven to 350° F.

Heat the olive oil in a large heavy pot. Add the carrots, celery and onion and stew them over medium heat, stirring occasionally, for 5 minutes; cover and cook an additional 5 minutes. Salt the pork. Remove the lid from the pot and add the pork, lemon slices, garlic, peppercorns, parsley, thyme, bay leaf, vinegar and stock or water. Bring to the simmer, place a piece of wax paper or parchment paper over the meat, cover with a lid and bake for 1½ to 1¾ hours. Turn the meat once as it cooks. Remove from oven and allow the meat, still covered, to cool in the liquid for at least ½ hour.

Remove the meat to a carving board. Discard the parsley, thyme branches and bay leaf. Drain off the liquid into a small metal bowl and thoroughly spoon off the fat that rises to the surface—you should have slightly more than 2 cups of broth. Season and reserve the cooked aromatic vegetables. Stir ½ cup of the cooking liquid into the softened gelatin, pour into a small saucepan and stir over low heat until heated through and the gelatin is thoroughly dissolved. Stir the gelatin mixture into the pork liquid and season to taste. Set the metal bowl in a larger bowl one-third full of ice water and stir the liquid until it begins to turn syrupy and is cold. Remove the bowl from the ice water and set aside.

Boil the peas in boiling salted water for 3 to 5 minutes, depending on the tenderness of the peas. Drain and refresh briefly in cold water. Drain thoroughly. Boil the new onions or tiny leeks in boiling salted water for 1 or 2 minutes (they will not really be cooked, only their surface rawness removed). Refresh and drain.

Remove the bone from the meat. Slice the pork and arrange it in a very large deep platter or white oval porcelain baking dish. Season the meat lightly with salt and pepper. Arrange the lettuce leaves around the edge so they extend above the rim of the dish. Spoon over the reserved aromatic vegetables, then the peas. Place the new onions or leeks around the platter. Pour over the cooled cooking liquid. Cover with plastic wrap and set in the refrigerator until ready to serve.

To serve, spoon pieces of the meat and soft jelly along with some of the vegetables onto plates.

SALT-RISING ROLLS

About 12 to 15 rolls

¼ pound potatoes, peeled and thinly sliced
2 cups boiling water
3 tablespoons nondegerminated cornmeal
2 teaspoons sugar
2½ teaspoons salt
6 to 7 cups unbleached all-purpose flour
1½ cups lukewarm milk
¼ teaspoon baking soda
4 tablespoons melted butter and 2 tablespoons for brushing

To make the starter, place the potatoes, boiling water, cornmeal, sugar and ½ teaspoon of the salt in a bowl and stir briefly. Set in a larger bowl of warm water and put in a warm place (at about 100° F.—a gas oven warmed by the pilot light or an electric oven turned on briefly every now and then is a good location) for 18 to 24 hours, until there is about a ½-inch layer of foam on the surface of the liquid. Replace the warm water occasionally as the starter develops. Remove the potatoes with a slotted spoon, rinse them over a bowl in a small amount of warm water, then discard them and add the rinse water to the starter liquid along with 3 cups flour, the milk and baking soda. Beat until smooth. Place again in a bowl of hot water in a warm place until the sponge (or starter) doubles in bulk, anywhere from 2½ to 3 hours.

In a large bowl stir together 2 cups of the remaining flour and the remaining 2 teaspoons salt. Add the sponge and the 4 table-spoons melted butter and beat until well blended. With your hands work in 1 cup more flour and turn the dough out onto a floured surface and knead for 6 to 8 minutes, adding additional flour as needed to make a smooth elastic dough. Shape into 12 to 15 balls about 2 inches in diameter, tucking and pinching the dough to-gether on the bottom of the ball to create a little surface tension and smoothness over the dough. Place 3 inches apart on 2 buttered baking sheets. Brush with the remaining 2 tablespoons melted butter; cover with a clean towel and set in a warm place to rise until nearly doubled in bulk, for 2 to 2½ hours. Bake in a preheated 350° F. oven for 14 to 18 minutes, until the rolls are lightly browned on top. Cool on a rack.

Note: If you wish to make loaves instead of rolls, divide the dough in half and shape into 2 loaves. Set in 2 buttered 8-inch bread pans, brush with butter and let rise as directed above. Bake in a 350° F. oven for 35 to 40 minutes. Cool on a rack.

CARAMELIZED BLACK WALNUT PIE

A 9-inch pie for 8

1½ cups heavy cream
¾ cup sugar
¾ cup maple syrup
2 eggs, lightly beaten
2 teaspoons vanilla extract
2 cups black walnuts, in large and small pieces
A partially baked 9-inch pie shell (follow the instructions on
*   page 272, baking the shell for only 15 minutes)*
Powdered sugar in a shaker

Preheat the oven to 400° F.

   Place the cream and sugar in a 3- to 4-quart heavy-bottomed saucepan and bring gradually to the simmer. Boil gently for 6 to 8 minutes, whisking occasionally and scraping the bottom of the pan, until the cream has caramelized slightly and is a light nut color (be sure to use a large enough saucepan or the cream, if reduced too rapidly, will boil over). Off the heat stir in the maple syrup, the eggs and vanilla. Add the black walnuts and stir well to coat them thoroughly with the caramelized custard mixture. Pour into the partially baked pie shell. Bake for 25 to 30 minutes, or until the custard is nearly set; do not overbake as the pie is best when the center is still slightly creamy. Cool on a rack for at least 1 hour; dust the edges with powdered sugar. Serve warm, with unsweetened lightly beaten cream if you wish.

8

THE FISH GOBBLER

New Orleans, Louisiana

Any man in chef's whites who would slink down the backstage corridor of Rosy's Jazz Club in New Orleans and, seeing Ella Fitzgerald's dressing room door ajar, slip into her room and into her street shoes to get the feel of greatness, while Ella was belting it out on stage—any man like *that* could only end up living across from Bad Estella's Shrimp Company on Burgundy Street in the Quarter. Joe Middleton did both those things—tried on the shoes and settled on slightly notorious Burgundy—because he liked situations that were rich. Ask Joe about safe and he'd fall asleep on you. Joe knew all about safe, growing up the son of an insurance claims adjuster in Texas. The Middleton household was decent enough: unwaveringly safe, undemonstrative, deathly dull. So Joe, who waltzed into life during a whopper storm in Corpus Christi in 1947, learned his creed early on. Brave the elements and life is rich. Scary sometimes, but rich.

Joe Middleton grew up craving riches and determined to avoid insurance. His first break came in Commerce, Texas, when he was eighteen and attending East Texas State University. Quickly enough college became incidental as El Sombrero ascended. El Sombrero was a 1960's-style Tex-Mex restaurant where Joe teethed as a cook, and it became the hangout for college kids in Commerce. They could drink beer there, they were free there, and when sweet-smilin'

97

Joe with the worried brown eyes fed 'em, he felt love he hadn't felt at home. The Middleton maternal instinct surfaced again in 1967 in Pearl Harbor, where as a Navy quartermaster in charge of operations for the Commander of Anti-Submarine Warfare Forces in the Pacific, Joe also operated Mother Hen's Sandwich Shop. When Joe wasn't shuffling maps and charting subs, Mother Hen's gave him another chance at culinary fulfillment.

Joe blossomed in Hawaii. Thrown in with officers and their wives, more receptive than enlisted men to culinary experiments, he cultivated new friends with food. Also during his three-year hitch on Oahu Joe began the exploration of Chinese cooking that was to color much of his later professional life. But more than Mother Hen's, or the bewitching flavors from Asia, one episode in Hawaii eclipsed all others and jolted Joe onto a new wavelength. One night he was dining with his division officer and his wife and was served: a boiled artichoke. Lights went off in Joe Middleton's head. In that greenish globe Joe savored all the yet untasted amazements of the planet, and resolved to make his life brave and new.

Around 1971 when he'd done with the Navy, Joe entered into serious culinary apprenticeship, that honored custom of transmitting excellence and guaranteeing the future integrity of professional kitchens through exposure to a master. Joe signed on with old-world hotel chefs, first in Chicago, then in Houston, and finally was drawn to the kitchens of Commander's Palace in New Orleans, where before too many months passed he began to weary of the succession of "thick-thumbed" chefs he had encountered. The devastating truth came to him: Apprenticeship is valueless if a master is not present. Joe panicked and retreated to Nature's Way, a blessedly artless health food restaurant where he could roam around the sprouts and contemplate his next flashing chance at bliss. If nothing else Joe was dogged; the advent of the artichoke had become a near cult with him. While the pleasant limbo of Nature's Way restored Joe, New York—distant, entrancing, promising—began its seduction. Finally in 1974, in the Great Metropolis, Joe found his first master, Anna Muffoletto. The prominent Italian cookbook author and cooking instructor sensed the bruises inflicted by a coarse school of thought—German hotel food—as well as Joe's yearning to be healed. Assisting Anna Muffoletto, cooking with her, watching her and tasting her food, Joe was exposed to craftsmanship, began forming his own food's soul.

When New York's work was done and had rekindled Joe's belief in himself and his craft, the honeyed lures of New Orleans drew him home. He eased into the Big Easy by signing on with the kitchen at Rosy's on Tchoupitoulas Street and pouring himself heart and soul into the last months of the jazz club's life. When it closed a few months later, Joe Middleton at the age of twenty-nine finally realized that he was ready to serve forth something of himself. He opened the Joe Middleton Catering Company and settled onto Burgundy Street across from Bad Estella's.

When I met him in 1979 that is where I found Joe, in the French Quarter cooking Chinese and cooking Italian and tending to his gray kitty-girl Itch. There was a hum and a happiness on slightly battered Burgundy Street. There was also a little fright every afternoon when the Fish Gobbler came to Bad Estella's to devour her daily disgorging of fish and shrimp debris. The mythical monster-truck first greedily inhaled all the shells and bones and cracked them up, smacking its gears, before swallowing them into its bottomless steel pit. Satisfied only after five or ten minutes of feasting, the Fish Gobbler then would rumble off, and Joe and Itch and everyone would grin. Afternoons with the Fish Gobbler, if a little fragrant, were rich.

THE FISH GOBBLER

Rosy's Oysters Rockefeller

Chicken with Walnuts

Carrots à la Sidecar

Anna Muffoletto's Chocolate Roll

———

The dishes in the following menu are all part of the Joe Middleton mosaic: saucy oysters from New Orleans, a little walnut chicken from China, a few boozy carrots à la sidecar (an homage to the French Quarter, where classic cocktails live on), and a fragile chocolate roll from Italy.

The Herbsaint in the oyster topping is an anise-flavored liquor similar to Pernod, and either can be used. Oysters Rockefeller, by the way, is delicious only if the oysters are absolutely freshly shucked, the spinach is fresh, and most importantly, if the oysters only bake long enough to be warmed through—nothing like the thick-thumbed variety we know so well.

Joe calls his walnut chicken "something to serve your most honored guest or food to fix when filled with love." The dish, with its two cups of shelled and skinned walnuts, is certainly an act of devotion. It can be vastly accelerated if you have helpers armed with bamboo skewers or toothpicks to pick off the skin. When walnuts are peeled, though, they are drastically altered: They lose any tannic (astringent) quality and will never be bitter. They are worth the work.

Anna Muffoletto's chocolate roll—made only with chocolate, eggs and sugar, and spread with cream flavored with Jamaican rum—is a real delicacy. Newfangled kitchens of the eighties and nineties often behave as if flourless chocolate cakes were a recent invention, but in fact, as Anna Muffoletto's cake from the sixties tells us, they've been around awhile.

P.S.: If any of these dishes appear greatly alcoholic, by the time they are finished they are not. Good food contains only the flavors, not the alcohol, of spirits.

ROSY'S OYSTERS ROCKEFELLER

Serves 6

6 *tablespoons butter*
3 *tablespoons finely chopped celery*
3 *tablespoons finely chopped scallions*
¾ *cup cooked fresh spinach, squeezed of any excess moisture*
3 *tablespoons finely chopped parsley*
⅓ *cup fine dry bread crumbs*
2 *tablespoons Herbsaint or Pernod*
Tabasco
Salt and freshly ground pepper to taste
3 *dozen freshly shucked oysters on the half shell, set on 2*
    baking sheets covered with a layer of rock salt

Preheat the oven to 500° F.

Melt the butter in a saucepan or skillet. Add the celery and scallions and cook over low heat for about 10 minutes, stirring occasionally. Add the spinach, parsley and bread crumbs and cook 5 minutes longer. Purée the mixture in a food processor or blender, add the Herbsaint or Pernod, Tabasco and salt and pepper to taste. Spoon or pipe with a pastry bag the green mixture over the oysters. Bake for 2 or 3 minutes, until the juices are just beginning to sizzle (the oysters should only be warmed through). Serve at once.

CHICKEN WITH WALNUTS

....

Serves 6

2 cups walnut halves
Peanut oil for frying
2 egg whites
Salt
3 tablespoons cornstarch plus 2 teaspoons cornstarch
1½ pounds skinned boneless chicken breast, cut into 1-inch
    pieces
Flour for dredging
¼ cup chicken stock
2 tablespoons soy sauce
1 tablespoon rice wine
1 teaspoon sugar
6 tablespoons safflower or corn oil
1 1-inch piece peeled fresh ginger, thinly sliced
1 cup broccoli flowerettes
1 cup snow peas, sliced in half

Drop the walnuts in boiling water and boil for 4 minutes; drain and while still damp peel away the brown skin with the help of a bamboo skewer or toothpick. Heat about ½ inch of peanut oil in a skillet or deep-fat fryer and when the oil is hot—about 375° F.— fry the walnuts in 2 batches for 30 to 40 seconds, or until they are golden. Drain on paper towels.

    Beat the egg whites with a pinch of salt until they are just stiff; beat in the 3 tablespoons cornstarch. Salt the chicken lightly and coat each piece with the egg white batter, then dredge in the flour. Fry the chicken pieces in the hot oil in which the walnuts were fried until golden, for about 1 minute. Drain on paper towels. (The dish can be done in advance up to this point.)

    Blend together the stock, soy sauce, wine, sugar and cornstarch. Heat the safflower or corn oil in a wok or large skillet. Add the ginger and sauté it gently for a minute or two to flavor the oil. Raise the heat to high and add the broccoli and snow peas, and stir-fry for a couple of minutes until the vegetables are almost done. Toss in the chicken pieces. Add the stock and rice wine glaze and stir over medium heat until the liquid simmers and has thickened. Add the walnuts and serve at once with rice if you wish.

CARROTS À LA SIDECAR

Serves 6

3 dozen baby carrots, peeled and rinsed
4 tablespoons butter
2 tablespoons Cointreau
⅓ cup lemon juice
¼ cup Jack Daniel's
¼ cup honey
Salt and freshly ground pepper to taste
Minced parsley

Preheat the oven to 350° F.

Boil the carrots in lightly salted water until tender (the length of time will depend on the size and quality of the carrots). Drain. In a small saucepan melt the butter, then whisk in the liqueur, lemon juice, bourbon and honey. Arrange the carrots in a buttered ovenproof dish just large enough to hold them in a single layer and season lightly. Pour the sidecar syrup over and bake for 15 minutes, basting the carrots occasionally. Sprinkle with the parsley and serve.

ANNA MUFFOLETTO'S
CHOCOLATE ROLL

■■■

A 14-inch roll for 8 to 10

8 ounces semisweet chocolate, broken into small pieces
3 tablespoons strong coffee
6 eggs, separated
½ cup granulated sugar
Vegetable oil
Powdered sugar, sifted
Unsweetened cocoa, sifted
1½ cups heavy cream
2 tablespoons Jamaican rum

Preheat the oven to 350° F.

Melt the chocolate with the coffee in a microwave oven or over low heat in a small heavy-bottomed saucepan; stir until smooth. Beat the egg yolks briefly, then gradually add the sugar and beat until pale yellow and fluffy. Beat the egg whites with a pinch of salt until they are stiff. Stir the chocolate mixture into the egg yolks, then fold in the egg whites.

Place a long sheet of wax paper over a lightly oiled 11 × 14-inch jelly-roll pan so that the paper extends 3 or 4 inches over each end. Lightly oil the top side of the wax paper. Pour the batter onto the paper, spreading it evenly. Bake the cake for 12 to 15 minutes, or until just set. Remove from the oven and press a damp cold towel on top of the cake and allow to cool for at least 20 minutes, longer if possible.

Spread two 16-inch overlapping pieces of wax paper on a flat working surface and sprinkle with a mixture of powdered sugar and cocoa in the approximate size and shape of the jelly-roll pan. Remove the towel carefully from the cake and run a spatula around the edges of the cake. Cut away any dry or slightly burned edges. Invert the cake onto the cocoa-and-sugar mixture and gently peel off the wax paper.

Whip the cream with the rum and a tablespoon or two of powdered sugar and spread over the cake. Roll up the cake, lifting the edges of the wax paper to fold the cake inward and start it rolling. Continue lifting the wax paper and roll the cake up gently and quickly and onto a large platter (don't worry if the cake breaks in places). Chill for at least 1 hour. Dust with powdered sugar and cocoa. Slice evenly with a serrated knife and serve.

9

....

DOT'S WHAMMY

Natchez, Mississippi

F loating a house down the Mississippi River in 1830 involved some risks. There were the usual sandbars and shallows, not to mention scoundrels, to reckon with, and also, assuming the house made it to port in Natchez, there was always the chance the whole thing would disappear off the dock. Unruly river things happened in Natchez in those days and a certain house-snatching, involving a barge owner's unpaid debt, was one of the unruliest. As Natchez city records show it, once the barge owner paid up, the house reappeared and continued the land portion of its journey over to Washington Street, where it settled onto its foundations and has resided placidly ever since.

Prefab houses were big news in antebellum Mississippi. Originating in Ohio, where lumber was plentiful and cheap, the first prefab houses, shipped in sections, made good sense to the more timber-sparse South. The beauty of the operation was that even the barges became houses too. Rather than send the empty barges back up against the big-river current, barge barons sent them down to New Orleans and dismantled them to make low-cost bargeboard houses. The sections of bargeboard were so tight they made some of the sturdiest and best insulated houses around.

As a married woman, Lee Barnes lived for a while in a bargeboard house on Apple Street in New Orleans. She also grew up in one of the three prefab houses still standing on Washington Street in Natchez, and she sometimes wondered, did the Apple Street barge-board float the Natchez homestead? No way to know, of course, but she wondered all the same. Lee liked questions of where and why. As a tomboyish school-kid growing up in Natchez in the fifties and sixties, she'd wonder things like: *where* shall I throw that foolish boy, in the trash can or lock him in the bathroom, and *why* do I have to sit in the principal's office all the time? Red-haired, freckle-faced Lee Barnes spoke in a high blur of soft racing words. She was kind of a rekindled Tom Sawyer, and an expert prankster in a time when kid pranks were basically harmless. Robert Barnes, Lee's father, didn't think it was so harmless though, when on the days he wasn't tending to his medical practice, he would venture out to inspect his precious walled garden with its winsome trellises of purple wisteria, and find crass watermelon vines marauding all over the place. No need to guess at the culprit; Dr. Barnes was a veteran of sweet Lee's tactics: suck on the watermelon, spit randomly and run. No fingerprints, an edible weapon, it was the prefect crime and it drove Robert Barnes wild.

How so sedate a household produced so daunting a child is somewhat of a mystery. Lee's parents, Bob and Bettina, both doctors, raised their children all the same, exposed them to good books and good food and encouraged in them good deeds. To be sure, Lee could behave when called upon to do so. She could put on a long dress with a hooped skirt and, without missing a beat, step out with her parents and four younger sisters to attend one of Natchez's parties. Most all the kids in Natchez owned dress-up outfits; little boys had tuxedos and little girls had long hooped skirts. Parties were important in Natchez; there was no other entertainment. And the children were always included. Dining out and dancing along-side their parents, they learned true manners and the rewards of warm fellowship. When not strafing the landscape with watermelon pits, kids in Natchez became good social beings.

Life was grand on the Natchez bluff. "We just owned the town, we could walk anywhere and feel perfectly safe and there was always stuff going on. And we were very creative—if there wasn't some-thing going on we made something go on." One of Lee's more demure accomplishments was rounding up a ukulele group when ukuleles suddenly became popular. On long summer afternoons Lee and her band would head down to the sandbars to inspect the Mississippi, stopping if they dared in notorious Natchez Under The Hill. The fabled settlement clinging to the Natchez bluffs was home to various shady characters—thieves and smugglers at least—and it made for daring expeditions. One day when the chimney on an old house in Natchez Under The Hill fell down, it was said that gold coins rained all over the ground. The Barnes gang never found any but returned frequently to continue the search, and the missing coin mystery became part of Natchez lore.

Worn out from her exploits, Lee always had the graceful mustard-colored house under the crêpe myrtles to pad home to, and that was the real good of a Natchez childhood. No matter what happened, you always had family and plenty of it. Living with the Barneses and their five girls was their great-aunt Atchie, who baked beautiful tea cookies, and who remained in the house until her death at the age of ninety-one. Old people lived to be really old in Natchez, and freedom from worry was one reason why (when you had troubles, you had family there to help). The other reason? Good food. In the Barnes house, meals gave the family its focus, and Dot Snell, the Barneses' cook, gave the family's spacious dining room focus in abundance. After thirty years the tastes of Dot's cooking are still with Lee: "Goodness gracious she made the best fried chicken. What did she do with it? Shook it in a bag with flour. We always had tons of fresh vegetables, mustard and turnip greens, and lady peas. I have no idea what those were, teeny field peas I guess. Dot would cook them with "seasoning meat"* and onion. And corn bread, Dot's corn bread was heavenly, she made it with flour and white cornmeal; the corn breads people made with cornmeal and no flour, Lord you could throw them and hurt somebody."

Dot's most famous dish was her seafood gumbo in which she cooked the okra until it was ropey and thickened the gumbo while giving it a browned okra flavor. Dot would add to her gumbo whatever good ingredients came along—shrimp, crayfish, crimson

---

*Salt pork.

late-summer tomatoes. Dot's Whammy, Lee called it. The Barneses ate two main meals a day—lunch and dinner. Leftovers never appeared on the table; Bob Barnes couldn't abide them, and wouldn't have his family eating them. It was the rule that leftovers could only appear in a Sunday gumbo. In the evenings after dinner Bob Barnes always loved a Frango Mint, a fine chocolate candy. The trouble was, his daughters had infallible noses for chocolate and no matter where Papa Barnes hid his candies, his daughters always unearthed them and polished them off. Striding smugly after supper to his latest cache for his daily Frango, Bob would open the box and find himself cleaned out. Fuming, he'd search for the gang leader. Nowhere to be found, of course. A swift job by the queen of hit-and-run.

Oh, growing up in Natchez was graceful all right. How could it be otherwise in a town with more old-South architectural finery than any place on earth? Good food, gentility, family ties—it was all there. Lee's a graceful grown lady herself now with babies and a husband, but that mustn't fool you. Scratch her and it's Natchez in the fifties again. Jerry Lee Lewis—born across the river in Concordia Parish—is firing up the airwaves, and little Lee Barnes, squinting down Washington Street, is ready for some scorching fun herself.

DOT'S WHAMMY

Dot's Seafood Gumbo

Buttermilk Biscuits (see page 268)

Boiled Rice   Green Salad

Ambrosia à la Natchez

Pecan Lace Cookies

Mrs. Mur Lee Anderson's Pralines

———

Lee Barnes took me home to Natchez in 1975. It was spring and the magnolias were in immense majestic bloom. The Barnes family threw a party and much of the town came, as well as guests from New Orleans and Baton Rouge. It was a lovely, lingering event. The house filled with people and in the evening the party spilled into the gardens hung with Chinese lanterns and scented with wisteria (and not a single fugitive watermelon vine in sight). Dot came out of retirement to make her gumbo, and after the feast there was a general flow of guests in pale dresses and dinner jackets along the glimmering streets of the bluff to Natchez Under The Hill, where we watched the moon in the Mississippi and caught the rowdy drift from the local catfish house at midnight. We were young, and laughing and murmuring we felt the tug of the wise old river.

I loved Dot's gumbo because it is gentle. It has no pork, no sausage, only shrimp, oysters and freshwater crayfish (if you can't get live crayfish, you can substitute 1 to 1½ cups fresh lobster or crab meat, and for the broth, use shells or other seafood trimmings). It has no spicy heat either, although hardened mouths might go for a few drops of Tabasco sauce (as you've likely guessed, I think that spicy heat, at least a noticeable amount of it, ruins good food). In the following recipe for Dot's gumbo, I have suggested olive oil as a substitute for bacon drippings for those who don't want animal fat in their food. While not typically Southern, olive oil is nonetheless an ingredient of warm places with a flavor that enhances earthy food. Dot's instructions for starting her gumbo read like this: "Chop lots of onions, the more the better. Brown onions in bacon drippings. Add okra (sliced), cook stirring until okra is mush and looks like a bunch of seeds. This takes forever." (It actually only takes about 50 minutes.) The gumbo crabs called for in the recipe are undersized crabs that in every other state but Louisiana you would have to throw back in the water. In Louisiana, though, they are prized for flavoring gumbo, and, although they don't really have any meat, you suck 'em if you're a good eater.

After the rich flavors of gumbo, ambrosia à la Natchez, an unsweetened orange and grapefruit salad with coconut, slaps your mouth awake and paves the way for buttery lace cookies and pralines.

A night in Natchez is not complete without pralines. Pop a few in your pocket, and you're ready for a stroll to the river.

DOT'S SEAFOOD GUMBO

Serves 6 to 8

2½ to 3 pounds live crayfish (or 1 to 1½ cups fresh lobster or crab meat)
1 cup chopped green onions plus 1 tablespoon for garnish
6 tablespoons bacon drippings or olive oil
2 medium onions, peeled and chopped
2 pounds okra, trimmed, washed and sliced
3 tablespoons flour
2 garlic cloves, peeled and minced
1 pound ripe tomatoes, cored and chopped
1 bay leaf
1 teaspoon fresh thyme leaves, or ½ teaspoon dried thyme leaves
6 gumbo crabs (optional)
1 teaspoon liquid crab boil (oil-based herb flavoring for gumbo) (optional)
2 pounds raw shelled shrimp
2 dozen small freshly shucked oysters
Salt and freshly ground pepper to taste
2 to 3 teaspoons filé powder
2 tablespoons chopped parsley for garnish

Blanch the crayfish in boiling salted water for 1 minute; drain, and when cool enough to handle remove the tail meat and set it aside. Simmer the crayfish heads and shells with 2 quarts water and the 1 cup chopped green onions for 30 to 40 minutes. Strain the crayfish broth and set aside. Heat 3 tablespoons of the bacon drippings or olive oil in a large heavy-bottomed pan. Add the onions and cook them over medium-high heat, stirring frequently, until they are lightly browned. Add the okra and cook, stirring frequently, over medium-high heat for 40 to 50 minutes; the okra should be mushy and look like a bunch of seeds.

In a small saucepan heat the remaining 3 tablespoons bacon drippings or olive oil over medium-low heat, add the flour and stir continuously until the *roux* is a deep, rich brown. Add the *roux* to the okra, then stir in the crayfish broth, garlic, tomatoes, bay leaf, thyme, the gumbo crabs and crab boil. Simmer for about 2 hours, stirring occasionally. (The gumbo may be done in advance up to this point.)

Just before serving, stir in the shrimp, oysters and reserved crayfish tail meat (or the lobster or crab meat). Correct the seasoning with salt and pepper. Either stir the gumbo filé into the hot gumbo (do not boil the mixture after the filé has been added or it will turn stringy) or place a small dish of gumbo filé on the table and allow each guest to add his or her own. Serve the gumbo sprinkled with parsley and the remaining chopped green onions over boiled rice.

Note: Filé powder, made from sassafras leaves, is used for thickening and flavoring Creole dishes. It can be found in the spice section of most markets.

does not set in the pan. When completely cool peel off the paper and store in an airtight container.

Note: It is important to emphasize that the hot mixture for Mrs. Anderson's pralines should begin to thicken and turn slightly granular while still in the pan; if the mixture remains smooth, the pralines will be chewy rather than melt-in-your-mouth crumbly and impossible to peel off the paper. Stirring the hot mixture briefly in the pan should give it just enough texture to set properly and yet still be liquid enough to run off the spoon (some people beat the mixture in the pan but this requires an expert eye as the hot sugar can overdevelop in a matter of seconds). As you form the pralines, if any remaining mixture begins to set in the pan, simply use two spoons to scrape it onto the oiled paper.

There's no denying that pralines are tricky. I've talked to the experts and they all agree: Even a seasoned praline-maker can have good days and bad days. But the experts also agree that pralines are always worth it. As Lee Barnes says, "There's nothing like a warm praline. I'd kill for warm pralines."

10

....

THE FAT STOCK
SHOW

Houston, Texas

Mary Ardeneaux could have grown up fretful but she didn't. Growing up in south Texas during the Depression and Dust Bowl days, sometimes in edge-of-town Houston and sometimes on the Gulf, back and forth between the two with a mother who couldn't settle, would have been enough to make any child edgy for life. But the little Ardeneaux girl never was. Good genes might have had something to do with it.

"The Ardeneaux bunch had a special gene. In addition to the green-eyed gene and the honey-brown hair gene, we've got that other one, the garlic gene. I guess it gave us good blood and a good outlook." The outlook shows in a quiet smile in a determined face. From where Mary now sits in Carmichael, California, black-eyed Susans and roses at her window, unwavering in the valley heat, the hardships of a Texas childhood appear worthwhile. They made the family sturdy.

Not that those twenties and thirties years were all grim. There was a charm to childhood on McKinney Street and the Ardeneaux kids—George, Leroy and Mary—all knew it. How many kids got to live across from the Fat Stock Show? Billie Ardeneaux settled there probably longer than she did anywhere else, and when she did her children went right to work making themselves known in the neighborhood.

123

With no dad around—George Ardeneaux died when Mary was one-and-a-half—everyone, with the exception of Mary, worked. Billie was a dressmaker and a furrier, and no matter where she was, her skills were always in demand by the "aristocracy" of Houston. Billie could take an evening dress bought at one of the downtown department stores and with a tuck or an extra seam give it that custom-tailored look. No one knew better than Billie Ardeneaux the craft of freshening a fur just out of its summer cold storage. Not that anyone needed furs in Houston, but those old coats, often in families for generations, were kept and coddled for the vanities of each new season.

While Billie, working out of the dingy apartment on McKinney Street, tended to the finery of fashionable Houston, her boys found after-school jobs in the neighborhood. They worked paper routes, and when the circus took over where the Fat Stock Show left off, they carried water for the circus animals. Mary didn't work. She was a girl and she was the youngest. So she just had fun. After school she would stroll over to the library at the curve in McKinney Street and read plays until dinnertime. The eight-year-old girl adored reading plays—*The Petrified Forest* was one of her favorites— and she loved looking at all the actors and actresses in the photographs. Mary was crazy for movies too. In the summer on McKinney Street there were outdoor movies in the park, complete with a piano player. Not having a personal income never stopped Mary from getting to that show. If she didn't have the nickel for her ticket, she'd zip around to the back of the nearby grocery and "borrow" a milk bottle from the bottle-rack. Back at home Mary would rinse the bottle out to give it that fresh-from-our-house look, then calmly walk it over to the grocery where, gleaming bottle backed up by gleaming smile, a nickel was handed over, and a little girl's enthrallment at the movies was guaranteed for one more night. Getting a little extra mileage out of those milk bottle deposits never seemed so bad. Sneaky maybe, but not so bad.

The circus and the movies weren't the only things that took the rough edges off of Depression-era life for the Ardeneaux family. Home life had some warmth to it too. The evening suppers drew them all together. Billie worked a full day, then cooked a good meal. It might have been simple—sparse even, sometimes—but it had that taste of home. Most often Mary, the only one not working, did the marketing. Some nights it was for no more than a "soup bunch"—beef bones placed on a square of butcher paper with two or three handfuls of week-old vegetables not good enough to sell but good enough for soup. That cost a quarter, and made into a thick soup, it gave a family a decent meal. Other nights it was a "long gravy" dinner, ground meat and rice with tomato-paste gravy. The gravy tasted good and it was a good thing, since there was usually more gravy than meat. On weekends Billie sometimes bicycled to one of the streams outside of Houston and caught catfish, which everyone loved dredged in cornmeal and fried. Once in a while a friend would arrive from a fishing trip on the Gulf Coast with a snapper or some small blue crabs that would be stuffed with cracker crumbs, onion and garlic—everyone craved garlic—then baked. Times were lean, but they weren't bland. Things tasted good.

Summers at Aunt Catherine's were something else that smoothed things over for the Ardeneaux family. Billie's sister Catherine and her husband worked the Treyhan cattle ranch about a hundred miles outside of Houston. He was the ranch foreman; she raised vegetables, milked the cows and cooked. They lived in a long, low, unpainted house surrounded by an unpainted picket fence—"houses in those days always needed paint, you'd paint the barn before you'd paint anything else." The house had a long verandah and was built up on posts, leaving a high space for when a gully-washer would hit. On dry summer days that space was cool, and the kids would scoot down there and play jacks.

For several summers in the early 1930's Billie Ardeneaux parked her children at her sister Catherine's. The kids fretted Billie sometimes, and besides, Houston in the summer was a den of bugs—polio was a threat then—and Billie knew Catherine would give good care to George and Leroy and Mary. Mary was happy during those summers. She was only seven or eight then, but summers with Aunt Catherine gave her a kind of certainty about things. There she was safe, and country life absorbed her. Never mind that the only sign of the outside world in all those miles of much, much ranch was the thin clatter of the train by the line of sassafras trees on the horizon, once in the morning and once at night. Those trains sort of framed the days, and the tracks were a frequent destination when the kids would spend all day riding, eating biscuit sandwiches and collecting sassafras root.

Mary and her brothers helped out on the ranch too, especially with the milking. Dressed unconventionally in overalls, Catherine was a fearless woman who faced a day's work with considerable momentum. The milk had to be in and strained, poured into the big metal milk cans and out on the road for pickup by seven A.M., and it always was. While the morning milking was going on, Catherine began breakfast. She got the wood stove heating and put the biscuits to rise, then fried the salt pork, supervised the milk straining, made the gravy and baked the biscuits, while one of the men got the milk on its way to the road. Then Catherine called everyone in. The men ate their breakfasts busily, then moved out into the day. The kids, though, dawdled, dunking their biscuits in the puddles of sorghum syrup and butter on their plates, asking for more biscuits, then more syrup—one always ran out before the other—until finally Catherine told them to scram.

Mary remembers the tastes of those summers as much as anything. Plain and abundant, food was a comfort, and Sunday at the ranch offered the most comfort of all. The day was slower, and the eating took longer. To enjoy Catherine's chicken and rolled dumplings, her sweet potato patties and tomato pudding, her coleslaw and greens, you needed a long afternoon. The whole week kind of aimed for Sunday, and if the kids took a walk on Saturday, you ate cobbler on Sunday. One of the prideful episodes of summer was bringing those blackberries home.

Sixty years later Mary doesn't pick berries much anymore. But that pride of family, from days in Houston or out at the ranch, is with her still. Like her mother, Mary was widowed very young; her own grown daughters live with her and she likes that. They may move away again, as they have before, but for the moment no one is worrying. The family still meets around the table, and though the gravy is not so long, the comfort is still there. But if the kids fret her, like kids do, Mary might ship them off to Texas and park them at her Aunt Catherine's for a month or two.

THE FAT STOCK SHOW

Garlic Chicken and Dumplings
with Long Gravy

Tomato Pudding

Turnips and Greens with Pot Likker

Sweet Potato Patties in Brown Butter

Black-eyed Peas with Whole Okra

Blackberry Cream Cobbler

———

Don't expect modern sense or science from a south Texas farm dinner. Expect instead sometimes sticky sometimes sweet always gentle tastes, one at a time in your mouth. The stickiness often comes from broth based on pork or chicken (the liquid cuts the fat so the dish is not really oily). The sweet softness comes not only from boosting the flavor of just-picked vegetables with sugar or sorghum, but also from the absence of sour tastes like vinegar or citrus. The softness also comes from thorough cooking; don't look for crisp at Aunt Catherine's.

All that said, the dishes in this menu are light and not really rich. I have leaned them up to some extent, and eased up on the sweetening in the tomato pudding. But the original flavors are there. Olive oil, because it has character, can work well as a substitute for pork fat, and I have suggested it in the black-eyed peas with whole okra. That dish is a good one for people who grimace at the thought of okra. When it is left whole and cooked only until tender, it does not become slimy and is delicious.

There are a lot of dishes in a menu like this; that's the way it's always been. One reason is that things don't cook in combination—farm cooking doesn't really like complication—and also, when dished up they make a fuller table. If a salad were served it would be simple sliced tomatoes in place of the tomato pudding, or maybe a coleslaw. Texas summer nights don't get cold enough to make heads of lettuce, and leafy salads were fairly unknown out in the south hills.

The chicken and dumplings have some unusual features, and are a good company dish because the skin and bones are removed once the chicken is cooked. The use of whole cloves of garlic is a real Ardeneaux touch; the garlic flavor, though, is delicate, as it poaches along with the dumplings. The cream in the broth is an optional finish, but a delectable one. A dish like this would traditionally have been made with a stewing hen, and if you can find one, increase the cooking time to 1½ to 2 hours. Rolled dumplings, it should be emphasized, are made with a stiffer dough than dropped dumplings and are necessarily chewier and not as fluffy; they are nonetheless excellent, and one of the traditions of the South.

Although there is no substitute for the woodsy flavor of wild blackberries, if there aren't enough around you could use raspberries or blueberries in the cobbler. Such measures might occasionally have been necessary at the Treyhan Ranch, since as Mary Ardeneaux tells it, "each kid brought back a quart bucket—*almost* full—spills and berry fights sometimes reduced our take."

GARLIC CHICKEN AND DUMPLINGS WITH LONG GRAVY

Serves 6

1 *large roasting chicken, 5½ to 6 pounds, or 2 3-pound fryers*
1 *carrot, scrubbed and coarsely chopped*
1 *celery stalk, washed and coarsely chopped*
1 *onion, peeled and sliced*
1 *bay leaf*
6 *garlic cloves, crushed slightly (cloves may be left unpeeled)*
2 *or 3 stems fresh thyme, or 1 teaspoon dried thyme leaves*
2 *or 3 parsley stems with leaves*
Salt and freshly ground pepper to taste
12 *garlic cloves, peeled*
Rolled Herb Dumplings (recipe follows)
¼ *cup heavy cream*
1 *teaspoon chopped fresh thyme leaves, or ½ teaspoon dried thyme leaves*
Whole flat or curly parsley leaves, rinsed and patted dry

Cut the chicken into serving pieces; place the wings, back, neck pieces and gizzard in a large pot with the carrot, celery, onion, bay leaf, 6 garlic cloves, thyme and parsley stems. Cover with water (about 3 to 4 quarts), add 2 teaspoons salt and bring to the simmer.

Cook the stock for 20 to 30 minutes, then add the chicken breasts, legs and thighs. Simmer the meat for 30 to 40 minutes, depending on the size of the pieces; if you prefer juicy white meat, cook the breasts a few minutes less than the dark meat. When the chicken is done, remove the pieces to a large ovenproof baking dish to cool slightly.

Strain the stock and degrease it thoroughly. Return the stock to the pot and reduce it over high heat by about half, to 5 to 6 cups. Correct the seasoning with salt and a good amount of pepper.

When the chicken is cool enough to handle, remove and discard the skin and the bones. If you have used the large roasting chicken, cut each piece into 3 smaller pieces; for the fryers, cut the breasts in half. Return the meat to the baking dish, and season lightly with salt and pepper. Spoon 5 or 6 tablespoons of the stock over the meat, cover snugly with foil and set aside (for not more than 1 hour at room temperature) before finishing the dish. (The chicken may also be refrigerated.)

Prepare the dumplings (see opposite). Preheat the oven to 250° F. About ½ hour before serving, place the chicken in the oven to rewarm if it has been refrigerated, but return it to room temperature first before placing it in the oven. Add the 12 cloves peeled garlic, then the dumplings to the stock brought back to the simmer, cover tightly with a lid and poach the dumplings for 18 to 20 minutes. Remove the lid, add the cream and thyme and correct the seasoning with salt and pepper. Spoon the dumplings and broth over the warm chicken. Garnish with the parsley leaves and some coarsely ground black pepper.

ROLLED HERB DUMPLINGS

18 to 20 dumplings

2 cups sifted unbleached all-purpose flour
1 tablespoon baking powder
¾ teaspoon salt
¼ teaspoon freshly ground black pepper
1 teaspoon chopped parsley
1 teaspoon chopped fresh thyme leaves, or ½ teaspoon dried
    thyme leaves
2 tablespoons unsalted butter
2 tablespoons vegetable shortening
½ to ⅔ cup milk

Stir together the dry ingredients with the parsley and thyme. Blend in the butter and shortening, using the tips of your fingers, until the mixture is in fine irregular crumbs. Stir in the milk with a fork, adding just enough liquid so that the dough forms a rough ball. Knead the dough 5 or 6 times on a lightly floured surface, then pat or roll it into a square approximately ⅓ inch thick. Cut out 1½- to 2-inch square dumplings (cut them so that there are no scraps; don't worry about even edges). If the dumplings are not to be poached immediately, cover them and set them aside, either at room temperature or in the refrigerator for a longer wait (allow the dumplings to return to room temperature before poaching).

TOMATO PUDDING

Serves 6

3 pounds ripe tomatoes, rinsed and cores removed
2 cups cubed bread (a less airy bread is preferred)
4 tablespoons butter, melted
¼ cup sorghum or molasses
¼ cup sugar
1 teaspoon salt
Freshly ground pepper to taste

Preheat the oven to 375° F.

Chop the tomatoes roughly either in a food processor or by hand. In a large bowl stir together the tomatoes with the remaining ingredients. Correct the seasoning with salt and pepper. Pour into a 2-quart baking dish and set in the oven for 45 to 50 minutes, or until the pudding is bubbling and the edges are slightly browned. Let cool briefly before spooning onto plates.

TURNIPS AND GREENS WITH POT LIKKER

Serves 6

4 ounces salt pork, cut into small strips
1 pound turnips, peeled and sliced
2 pounds turnip greens, thoroughly washed and drained, stems
    trimmed
Salt and freshly ground pepper to taste

Place the salt pork in 1 quart cold water, bring to the simmer and cook gently for 30 minutes. Skim the liquid frequently. Add the turnips and cook until tender, 5 to 10 minutes (depending on the thickness). Add the greens and boil another 4 or 5 minutes. Correct the seasoning with salt and pepper.

Drain the pork, turnips and greens (reserve the liquid) and place on a platter or in a serving bowl. Pour about 1½ cups of the liquid—the "pot likker"—over the greens and serve. Any leftover pot likker is good poured over corn bread.

SWEET POTATO PATTIES
IN BROWN BUTTER

Serves 6

4 cups cold puréed, cooked sweet potatoes (about 3½ pounds raw)
2 eggs, lightly beaten
1½ teaspoons salt
Freshly ground pepper to taste
¼ teaspoon freshly grated nutmeg (optional)
1 cup crushed nonsweet crackers
5 or 6 tablespoons butter

Stir together the sweet potato purée, eggs, seasonings and nutmeg. Using floured hands, pat the sweet potato mixture into patties about 3 inches in diameter and ½ inch thick (depending on the potatoes, it can be soft and a little messy to handle). Roll the patties in the cracker crumbs and lay them out on a baking sheet. Melt 3 tablespoons butter in a large skillet and cook the butter over medium heat until it has browned slightly and has a delicate nutty aroma. Cook the patties in the brown butter for about 2 minutes on each side, until they are nicely browned; add more butter as necessary to the pan in between batches, and brown it. Drain the patties on absorbent paper and serve. (The patties may be browned an hour or two in advance, placed in a large shallow baking dish and reheated at the last minute in a preheated 450° F. oven for 4 or 5 minutes.)

BLACK-EYED PEAS WITH WHOLE OKRA

Serves 6

2 tablespoons bacon drippings or olive oil
½ cup finely chopped onion
1 bay leaf
1 teaspoon salt
Freshly ground pepper to taste
1 pound fresh or frozen black-eyed peas
½ pound fresh okra, left whole, tops trimmed

Heat the bacon dripping or oil in a large saucepan, add the onion and stew gently for 5 minutes. Add 3 cups water, the bay leaf and seasonings, bring to the boil, add the black-eyed peas and simmer for 20 minutes. Add the whole okra and continue to cook another 5 to 10 minutes, according to the size of the okra, until it is tender but not mushy. Correct the seasoning with salt and pepper, remove the bay leaf and serve.

BLACKBERRY CREAM COBBLER

▪▪

Serves 6 to 8

6 cups fresh wild blackberries
¾ to 1 cup sugar, depending on the sweetness of the berries,
*   plus 2 tablespoons*
2 tablespoons plus 2 cups unbleached all-purpose flour
½ teaspoon salt
1 tablespoon baking powder
1 tablespoon vegetable shortening
6 tablespoons butter
1 cup heavy cream
Powdered sugar in a shaker

If you must, rinse the berries briefly, and drain them, but it is better not to (washing delicate berries washes away their flavor). In a large mixing bowl toss together the berries with the ¾ cup sugar, the 2 tablespoons of flour and a pinch of salt. Place in a 10- to 12-cup shallow ovenproof glass or porcelain dish (or a metal pan as long as it is not aluminum).

Preheat the oven to 400° F.

Stir together the 2 cups flour with the remaining salt, baking powder and the 2 tablespoons sugar. Using the tips of your fingers, blend in the shortening and 4 tablespoons of the butter, working until the mixture resembles coarse bread crumbs. Stir in the cream with a fork, adding any extra drops of cream necessary to gather up any dry bits and form the dough into a ball. Knead the dough 3 or 4 times on a lightly floured surface, then roll it out into the shape of whatever baking dish you have chosen. Pinch an attractive pattern around the edge of the dough. Dot the berry mixture with the remaining 2 tablespoons butter. Place the dough over the berries— it is fine if the dough does not completely cover them, the fruit is pretty when it shows around the edges and also the open edge will allow more steam to escape. Cut several deep slashes in the dough for steam vents. Bake the cobbler for 25 to 30 minutes; the fruit juices should be bubbling and the crust a light brown. Cool for 10 to 15 minutes, dust with powdered sugar, and serve with a little plain unbeaten cream on the side.

11

QUEEN ESTHER

Pawhuska, Oklahoma

Billy Cross can remember the first time he saw Queen Esther. Actually he remembers the first time he heard her name. Billy was ten when he started hearing his parents and their friends talk about Queen Esther. He thought that she was some exotic character out of the Bible; and she was.

One day Billy's dad Buddy hollered at him, "Come on, Billy, we're going ridin' to eat some of Queen Esther's fried pheasant and sweet corn hash." Billy was not thrilled at the prospect of going riding, especially in one of the coldest winters in thirty years. But he reluctantly got into his dad's '55 Chevy pickup and off they went to Pawhuska, the county seat of Osage County in northwestern Oklahoma.

Buddy Cross had married a woman from Pawhuska and he never let his wife forget that he himself was not from Oklahoma. He was from Kansas and somehow felt that he was a step above the Okies even if he was raised, and lived with his wife and two sons, only two miles north of the Oklahoma border in Chautauqua Springs, Kansas. But when it came to food, Buddy Cross kept his opinions about Oklahoma to himself and chowed down.

As Billy and his father crossed from Kansas into Oklahoma that winter day of 1956, Billy automatically licked the closed fist of his left hand and slapped it with the open flat palm of his right hand.

His maternal grandmother, Grace McKenzie, taught all of her grandkids the special good luck movement that always had to be done whenever they crossed into Oklahoma with or without her. Buddy ignored his son's quickly done suspicious hand movement, sucked on his cigarette and goosed the Chevy truck on down the road and into the red dirt rolling-hill country that was the ancestral homeland of the Osage Indians.

When Billy first saw Queen Esther she was standing in front of the biggest stove he had ever seen. It was a six-burner enamel gas monster, with an additional four burners to the left in black cast-iron that were fired by wood. Each stove had a corresponding oven, deep and wide, floating below the flaming stove tops.

Esther was big. She was wide and she was tall. One did not get the impression that she was fat, she was just big. She was also the blackest black person the quiet red-headed boy from south Kansas had ever seen. That is why he knew she was a Queen and that she was that Queen from the Bible. She was so black and so big and so in command of that stove that everyone approaching her kitchen that day took off his hat and slightly bowed when greeting her.

Buddy Cross, who had known Queen Esther for twenty years, called out to her that it sure did smell good. She said something about his being born hungry, and then she slightly turned around and smiled this big gleaming smile, with black eyes glistening and the perspiration beading along her hairline underneath a sunlight-white kerchief tied around her head. She was the Queen, and father and son both knew it. Her scepter was a very long wooden-and-steel kitchen fork with which she was turning the frying cut-up pheasants that were bubbling away in gigantic cast-iron skillets. She was cooking the birds in bacon fat and unsalted home-churned butter. As she was turning the pieces with her left hand, she was salting and peppering and flouring more pieces of pheasant with her right hand, and adding them to the skillets.

Using her right knee, she would pull at the side of the door handle of the big oven and check on the corn bread. To her left in the wood-burning oven she was baking apple pies. Queen Esther never baked pies in anything except a wood oven because she thought that gas was no good for pies. And electricity, my God no.

Electricity was for people who did not know how to eat, much less cook.

She had a big table in the middle of the kitchen that was laid out with the prettiest white china with gold rims. It was so thin you could see through it (almost). The table linens were white cotton and heavily starched, with napkins that looked more like bedsheets than napkins.

Some time in the afternoon, but before dusk, someone poured half water-glass tumblers of homemade applejack whiskey, and after a while two of the biggest platters of creamy, crunchy chicken-fried pheasant appeared on the table, along with big slabs of white corn bread passed with pan gravy, sweet corn hash, pan-fried tomatoes, buttered peas and pearl onions and towering flaky-crust apple pies. His grumblings about winter forgotten, Billy dragged his chair close to the table.

Billy grew to be a man, but he never forgot Queen Esther, who became his friend and taught him how to make white cake and iron a white dress shirt, both of which he can do to this day and prefers to do himself.

QUEEN ESTHER

Oklahoma-fried Pheasant
with Pan Gravy

Sweet Corn Hash

Pan-fried Tomatoes

White Corn Bread

Flaky Apple Pie

Straight Shots of Applejack
and
Black Coffee

———

In traditional Oklahoma cooking, a fried fowl dinner would usually have involved the use of some rendered bacon fat. For a richer flavor, some or all of the cooking oil recommended for frying Queen Esther's pheasant or her tomatoes in the following recipes may be replaced with bacon fat. Either way, pheasant or any other fowl fried Oklahoma-style is a great delicacy. There is no batter involved, only a light dusting with flour, which gives a melting and crisp result. There are no flavorings included other than, in addition to salt, the generous use of freshly ground pepper on the fowl and in the pan gravy—one of the unwavering characteristics of true Oklahoma flavor. Some pheasant cooks like to alternately fry and steam their birds as they cook, and this is accomplished by placing a lid over the skillet for 2 or 3 minutes several times during long slow cooking. This method produces very creamy fowl, with a rather less crunchy skin. It is also a somewhat refined skill and requires some practice to get it right.

In the nonsummer months, the sweet corn hash is a useful dish since it makes something flavorful of off-season corn. The same can be said of the tomatoes. In the summertime, the fried tomatoes could certainly be replaced by thick slices of beefsteak tomatoes, salted and peppered and parslied and eaten as a salad.

There is always a controversy about sweetness in corn bread. Queen Esther liked her corn bread with a faint amount of sugar to mellow the cornmeal. Buttermilk in the batter helps make it fluffy.

Among fruit pie bakers, those with the wisest touch make their pies plain. If the fruit has good flavor, they don't muddy it with spice; if the fruit is juicy, a little thickening helps, but too much makes a clumsy pie. Just some butter dotted over the fruit, that combines with the sugar and fruit juices to make them soft and syrupy—that's often the best thickening. As for good pie crust, the one here is one of the flakiest around. It contains no butter, and doesn't need to. Queen Esther's apple pie has no shiny glaze either, just the dry and golden blisters that tell you, at a glance, that here is someone who really knows about pie.

OKLAHOMA-FRIED PHEASANT WITH PAN GRAVY

■■

Serves 6

Vegetable shortening or oil for frying
Salt and freshly ground pepper to taste
6 pounds fresh pheasant, cut up
¾ cup flour plus 2 tablespoons for the gravy
2 cups milk, or 1 cup each milk and evaporated milk

Place a couple of heavy skillets over medium heat and add the shortening or oil (there should be about ¼ inch of fat in the pans for frying). While the pans are heating, salt and pepper both sides of the pheasant pieces. In a roasting pan or large mixing bowl stir together the ¾ cup flour, 1 teaspoon of salt and some additional fresh pepper. Toss the pheasant in the flour mixture until all the pieces are evenly coated.

When the oil is hot (a piece of pheasant should begin to sizzle gently when placed in the pan) add the pheasant pieces and fry them for 25 to 30 minutes, depending on the size of the pieces and the actual temperature of the oil. Turn the pieces of pheasant several times as they cook; if you wish, remove the breasts 3 or 4 minutes before the dark meat if you prefer very juicy breast meat. The pheasant should be a medium golden brown when it is done (if you cook it too quickly it will be too dark). Remove the pheasant from the pan, pressing each piece with a pair of tongs and squeezing it briefly over the skillet to remove any remaining oil. Set on a tray lined with paper towels before arranging on a platter. The fried pheasant is good hot, warm or cold, but is at its best if eaten within a half hour of being fried.

Pour off all but 3 to 4 tablespoons of the fat and browned drippings in one of the skillets. Place the pan over medium-low heat and stir in the 2 tablespoons flour. Cook the flour, stirring constantly, for 3 to 4 minutes. Pour in the milk and whisk the mixture steadily until the gravy comes to the simmer, has thickened and is smooth. Correct the seasoning with salt and a good amount of fresh pepper. Simmer for a few minutes; serve the pheasant and pass the gravy with the corn bread (see page 146). (The gravy can be made in advance and rewarmed; thin it with a few tablespoons of additional milk, when reheating, if it seems necessary.)

SWEET CORN HASH

Serves 6

6 tablespoons butter
5 cups fresh uncooked corn kernels, cut off the cob with a knife
    (about 7 or 8 ears)
Salt and freshly ground pepper to taste
1 to 2 tablespoons dark molasses

Melt the butter in a large skillet or saucepan set over medium heat. Add the corn, season lightly, and stir or toss the corn to coat with the butter. Cook the corn, depending on its tenderness, for 4 to 6 or 7 minutes, stirring occasionally. You may cover the pan with a lid for part of the time to steam the corn and help it cook evenly. Add the molasses to taste halfway through the cooking. Correct the seasoning with salt and pepper and serve.

PAN-FRIED TOMATOES

••

Serves 6

1½ pounds tomatoes, washed and cut into ½-inch slices
Salt and freshly ground pepper to taste
Flour for dredging
Cooking oil

Season the tomatoes with salt and fresh pepper; dredge them lightly with the flour. Pour ⅛ inch of oil into a large skillet set over medium-high heat. When the oil is hot, add enough tomato slices to fill the pan without crowding. Brown the tomatoes on both sides, and remove them when the outer edge is easily pierced with a knife. Repeat with the remaining slices. Serve hot with the pheasant.

WHITE CORN BREAD

••

Serves 6

1 cup white cornmeal
1 cup flour
¾ teaspoon salt
2 teaspoons baking powder
½ teaspoon baking soda
1 tablespoon sugar
⅓ cup corn or safflower oil plus 2 tablespoons for the skillet
1 egg, beaten lightly
1 cup buttermilk

Preheat the oven to 400° F.

Stir together the dry ingredients. In another bowl blend together the ⅓ cup oil, egg and buttermilk. Stir the liquid ingredients into the cornmeal mixture, mixing until just moistened and the larger lumps are broken up; don't overmix. Place the 9-inch ovenproof skillet over medium heat and pour in the 2 tablespoons oil. Tilt the pan in all directions to coat the bottom and sides evenly. When the oil is hot, pour in the batter. Bake for 20 minutes. The corn bread should be a light golden brown in the center and around the edges. Cool for 10 to 15 minutes before cutting into wedges either directly from the pan, or unmolding onto a round platter.

FLAKY APPLE PIE

For 1 10-inch pie serving 8

3 pounds tart green apples, peeled, cored, and cut into ½-inch
   slices
Grated zest of 1 lemon
1 teaspoon lemon juice
⅔ to ¾ cup sugar, depending on the tartness of the apples
1 to 2 tablespoons flour, if the apples are very juicy (optional)
2 tablespoons butter
10-inch pie plate lined with Pie Dough (recipe follows)
12-inch round of pie dough for the top

Preheat the oven to 450° F.

In a mixing bowl toss the apples with the lemon zest and lemon juice, then stir in the sugar and optional flour. Mound the fruit evenly in the pie plate and dot with the butter. Moisten the edges of the dough with a little water, then place the top piece over the fruit and fold the edges under as you press them together to seal. Pinch an attractive border onto the edge of the dough, then cut steam vents in the top of the pie. Place on the bottom of the oven for 10 minutes. If you are using a gas oven, it is a good idea to set the pie on a baking sheet and then on the very bottom of the oven, to begin baking the bottom crust before the juices start to run (if you are using an electric oven, set the baking sheet on the very bottom shelf). When the pie has begun to brown slightly, lower the temperature to 400° F., place the pie still on its baking sheet on a middle oven rack and bake for an additional 40 to 45 minutes, until the top crust is golden brown and the apples are very tender when pierced with a knife. Cool for at least 2 hours before serving. Baked fruit pies are actually best served at room temperature, or only faintly warm.

PIE DOUGH

To make 1 10-inch 2-crust pie

2¼ cups unbleached all-purpose flour
¾ teaspoon salt
¾ cup solid vegetable shortening
5 or 6 tablespoons cold water

Stir together the flour and salt. Blend in the shortening, using the tips of your fingers, until you have a rather coarse mixture with small pieces of shortening, about the size of corn kernels, remaining. Do not overmix. Stir in the water and form the dough into a ball. Gather up any dry bits of flour mixture at the bottom of the bowl using drops of water to make them stick together. Divide the dough in half and roll it out about ⅛ inch thick on a lightly floured surface.

12

THE LEMON JELLY CAKE

Tory, Illinois

Anyone living in central Illinois who was stricken with palsy of the stomach in the year 1900 had a choice. He could drive over to Chicken Bristle and let that new doctor over there tend to his woes. Or—by far the surer route—he could head straight for Tory and hope that nice Dr. Bradford would be in his office, and not off along with half the town at the annual Horse-Thief Picnic. That picnic was actually the Antihorse-Thief Picnic, but after a few years' worth of picnics no one bothered with the "anti" anymore, no one cared what you called a picnic as long as there was plenty of fried chicken. Anyway, even if Dr. Bradford wasn't in, there was always his daughter Helene. On that picnic day in 1900 with hardly a soul in town except young Helene Bradford, who had stayed home to keep her best friend Gracie company, the telephone rang—which was an adventure in itself; there weren't many phones in Tory—and it was Mrs. Blankenbarger in deep distress. In a hoarse whisper she confirmed the worst: She had drunk some milk from her old Jersey cow Queenie and sure enough, what with her palsy and all, the rich milk had churned to butter in her stomach. Moaning on her bed, she could feel the lump just as plain, and knew she'd have to be cut.

That turn-of-the-century summer in Tory, Illinois, was a summer of endless amazements, and they had come so fast that eleven-year-old Helene had finally given up and stopped counting. First there had been the arrival in their lives of Mr. Fenton, the kind man from Chicago who had been to Paris and did worldly things and who wrote long letters to Helene's mama, Kate. Then there was Helene's beautiful birthday party with the Chinese lanterns Mr. Fenton had brought from the city, which had erupted into turmoil with the abduction from the supper table of Mrs. Antha's pink angel food. The cloud of mystery and suspicion surrounding *that* event hung over Tory for days and eventually settled into the currents of local legend. And now Helene was facing the most amazing moment of all: She was going to have to save Mrs. Blankenbarger's life. She felt lucky she'd heard her papa discussing the case the week before, because that had given her time to think up a cure (one that didn't involve cutting). Helene knew that hot coffee would melt butter, she and her papa dunked toast in their coffee when there wasn't company around. The hunks of butter floated off in flat yellow patches. Kate Bradford despised this practice, but her husband said that "home was where you could do as you pleased, and if it wasn't, that damn-fool motto *Home Sweet Home* had better be taken off the wall."

Armed with her cure, Helene finally had the chance to perform a heroic act. Helene needed one of those to her credit after the debacle of the bluing, when Helene's mama and Mrs. Antha had been plotting how to out-pickle Minnie Overstreet at the State Fair, and, wondering if bluing could be safely used to make the blue layer of red-white-and-blue cabbage pickles, they had sent Helene off to consult her papa. Somehow Helene had gotten the words garbled and Dr. Bradford had flown up the street in a froth thinking his wife had swigged bluing. So now off Helene sped with a can of coffee and her mother's white granite coffeepot to save Mrs. Blankenbarger's life. And, after choking down some of the scalding black potion, Mrs. Blankenbarger *was* better, and she sat up and pronounced herself "well enough to kill and fry a chicken for Sam's supper when he gets home. That Effie Baldwin couldn't fry a decent chicken." Flushed from a good day's doctoring, Helene probably missed the heat in Mrs. Blankenbarger's newly revived voice. After all, while his wife was home churning butter in her bowels, what was Sam Blankenbarger doing out at the Horse-Thief Picnic with Effie Baldwin anyhow? As it turned out, that was one of the questions that hovered over that Tory summer.

A lot of people would have called Helene bold for shouldering, even only for an afternoon, the burdens of the medical profession. Her father called her a few things more when he heard the story, but a scolding wasn't anything that a bowl of frozen cream next door at Mrs. Antha's wouldn't fix. Mrs. Antha was gruff but goodhearted, and her remedy for any crisis was to eat or drink. "Gracie, now you eat a lot," she'd say, "you've got legs like toothpicks. And look at you, Helene, your eyes look like burnt holes in a blanket. You'd better eat a lot too. Will!" she'd bark at her husband. "You watch the girls' dishes and keep 'em filled." Moving the cookie plate nearer she'd mutter, "Just as I said. Burnt holes in a blanket."

If Mrs. Antha dispensed comfort with her rich and crumbly cookies, and competed somewhat peevishly with her pickles, she reigned with her cakes. Cakes were the real currency of Tory. Oh, townsfolk might have bartered with cabbages and sausages, and outdone each other with bronzed lawn ornaments and gilded rolling pins in the parlor, but if you baked cakes you had clout. And Mrs. Antha baked cakes: raspberry jam cakes, and her mythical, float-out-of-the-oven angel food. Mrs. Antha's angel food cake was so coveted around town she kept the recipe hidden in the clock on the mantel, safe from any passing snoops in the possible employ of Minnie Overstreet. Kate Bradford, on the other hand, baked probably the most illustrious cake of all, her lofty four-layer lemon jelly cake, and no one had to snoop for her recipe, she just trusted people to ask for it. The thing was, not a lot of folks did, since the cake was intricate and, to put it in the words of Mr. Fenton, no one could make it as pretty as pretty Kate Bradford. Mrs. Antha and Kate Bradford were cake royalty around Tory; the day Mr. Fenton gave Kate an "icing look," Helene knew there was more than just cake love between her mama and the polished man from Chicago. But, in those days, icing looks often stopped with the look. Helene was relieved about that. After all it was the twentieth century, and the best of all possible worlds.

■   ■   ■

Madeline Babcock Smith pushed back from her desk and rubbed her eyes. The pages looked plump and satisfying; the last layer of *The Lemon Jelly Cake* was almost in place. Just as well, that fine editor over in Boston, John Woodburn, was eager for the manuscript. The year 1952 was going to be a good one: her first book in print by August. In the meantime it was a spring evening in Rochester, Illinois—like Tory, a town so small it pinched—and time for a pickup supper with her brood. There'd be cold fried chicken, and some canned salmon with parsley and lemon, and maybe a compote of pink hard-boiled eggs which Mrs. Antha had colored by. . . . Madeline Smith smiled to herself. There was no Mrs. Antha. And no Tory. Nor any palsy of the stomach. Except in the plump pages of her book, thank goodness for those. But there sure was lemon jelly cake, wasn't there a good wedge of it, four layers high, sitting down in the icebox.

THE LEMON JELLY CAKE

Kate Bradford's Lemon Jelly Cake

Kate Bradford's lemon jelly cake is delicate and tall. The lemon jelly itself is nothing more than homemade lemon curd, spread between the layers. While the thick meringue makes a sweet and not-so-rich frosting, in the summer serving the cake chilled with a frosting of lightly sweetened whipped cream with a little vanilla would be a refreshing change.

KATE BRADFORD'S LEMON JELLY CAKE

A 4-layer, 8-inch cake for 12 to 15

1 cup unsalted butter at room temperature
1½ cups sugar plus ½ cup for the egg whites
3 cups sifted cake flour
3½ teaspoons baking powder
1½ cups milk
1 teaspoon vanilla extract
8 egg whites at room temperature
½ teaspoon salt

Preheat the oven to 375° F.

Lightly butter and flour four 8-inch cake pans. Working with a wooden spoon or an electric mixer, cream the butter, then add the 1½ cups sugar, beating until the mixture is fluffy. Sift the flour again with the baking powder and add it alternately with the milk to the butter and sugar mixture, beating until smooth after each addition. Add the vanilla. Beat the egg whites with the salt until they begin to form soft peaks. Gradually add the remaining ½ cup sugar and continue beating until the whites are fairly stiff. Stir a large spoonful of the whites into the cake batter, then fold in the remaining whites. Do not overmix. Divide the batter among the cake pans and smooth it evenly to the sides. Bake for 18 to 20 minutes; the layers should be light brown and just beginning to pull away from the sides of the pan. Cool the pans for 20 minutes on racks, then invert the layers onto the racks to finish cooling.

THE LEMON JELLY FILLING

10 egg yolks
1¼ cups sugar
Pinch of salt
Grated rind of 1 lemon
½ cup lemon juice
6 tablespoons unsalted butter

Place all the ingredients in a heavy-bottomed nonaluminum saucepan (aluminum can make egg yolks turn green). Place the pan over medium-low heat and stir constantly until the mixture nears the simmer and has thickened. Do not boil. Remove from the heat and continue stirring to cool the mixture. Pour into a bowl and allow to cool completely at room temperature.

For the cooked meringue frosting

¾ cup sugar
¼ cup water
2 egg whites
Pinch of salt
¼ teaspoon cream of tartar
1 tablespoon water

In a small saucepan boil the sugar and ¼ cup water for 1 or 2 minutes, until the sugar syrup runs in a slow stream off the end of a spoon and the last drops are sticky. In a bowl beat the egg whites with the salt, cream of tartar and 1 tablespoon water until they form soft peaks. Gradually add the boiling sugar syrup to the egg whites, beating at high speed until the meringue is stiff and shiny. Set aside to cool.

To assemble the cake, spread the cooled cake layers with the lemon jelly and place them on top of each other. Frost with the thick meringue. The cake is good served either at room temperature or chilled.

13

....

HOG HOLDER

Shelbyville, Indiana

If an eleven-year-old Indiana kid could wrestle cattle and not bat an eye, he sure could hold 1,400 pigs a day and not get worn out. And at a dime a pig, Brian Barlow held those pigs and held them gladly. Shelbyville, Indiana, was rife with swine in the 1950's. Pork for profit was burgeoning—compared to cattle, pigs multiplied fast and got fatter on less—and Kentucky was happy to ship its hog surplus north to Shelbyville into the open arms of local farmers. Being the local veterinarian and the local veterinarian's son meant you got cracking during hogging time. At least processing young eighty-pound pigs—vaccinating them against erysipelas and relieving the boy pigs of their boyish parts—was manageable. A kid could get his arms around a six-month-old porker and hold him tight while his dad poked around. Later on, though, those same dainties would balloon into colossal swine, a thousand pounds or more. The Hoosiers grow them big, just like they grow them tall.

Something else they grew in Shelbyville was fast cars (and if the cars weren't fast the drivers were). Located in the shadow of the Indy 500 as Shelbyville was, kids didn't exactly grow up enamored of go-carts. Rolling iron had a supremacy on the Indiana landscape probably only surpassed by the steady presence of silos. Growing Hoosier boys needed prospects other than pigs, and the idea—if not the fact—of muscle cars was pretty alluring. Of course if your

161

family didn't actually own a muscle car, a 1962 Plymouth wagon was a potent enough substitute, at least it was for a (by then) fourteen-year-old, six-foot-three-and-climbing local boy. So when Shelbyville shimmied on Saturday night, the heavy cruisers came out and Brian Barlow and his pal Sam Schaf cruised with the best of them. Starting at the Starlight Cafe, down Main Street past the Big Boy, as far as the A&W and back again, that was as far as daring stretched in those days. Anyone still unscathed after that itinerary and giddy with the adrenaline of the unapprehended would head for the levee, where bully charges over the crests of Peanut Hill induced stunning flights of heavy metal. The local body shops thought highly of Peanut Hill. But did the restless youth of Indiana respect the legal driving age out in Shelbyville in the 1960's? Hell no.

There was a kind of split life in Shelbyville back then, half town and half country. The Barlows were townspeople who, though they weren't farmers, lived close to the land. Brian had his daily work with the animals, birthing calves and trimming cattle horns and sweeping the kennels (Brian learned not to bring home schoolwork: With an exacting veterinarian father, you cultivated speed at school and a state of preparedness at home). Helping doctor livestock and pets consumed much of the oldest Barlow boy's childhood.

There were high times too with his greatgrandad Artist (that's his first name) Preston Fox who lived at one end of the Barlow compound in a converted chicken coop, a *nice* chicken coop that had made a tidy cottage. Greatgrandpa Fox liked jokes—without television (Brian's dad despised TV) you needed something, so the old man joked and teased and even conversed with the kids, and having brains not numbed by the numbing networks, the kids enjoyed that conversation. Greatgrandpa Fox also liked fishing, and he and Brian would zoom off to the Blue River in his 1939 V-8 Ford coupe and go angling for sunfish and catfish and bluegill. At the end of the day, watching the loaded boat-trailer drag the black coupe into the river as Greatgrandpa Fox gave 'er the gun and tried to transcend mud and gravity was just as much fun as fishing. Brian loved hooting at the old man who, most times, was the one hooting at him. Those fishing trips meant a lot to the gleeful Barlow boy-giant. But so, too, did the high torque siren-call that surged over the soybean fields from Indianapolis to Shelbyville and set town streets and a youth's heart to smoldering.

To be honest, Shelbyville may have been incendiary a few nights here and there, but on the whole things were pretty calm. Farming was everything, even if you weren't a farmer. Putting good into the earth and taking good out, that was the real prospect of rural Indiana. It was greatly accomplished with family members and neighbors all pitching in: Farm machines were expensive and not so plentiful in the fifties and sixties, and farms succeeded on the basis of extended family. And if you weren't a farm family, often you hired out to one. By the time he reached college-age Brian had worked countless hay harvests and was a master silo builder. Unlike grain-oriented places like Kansas, where silos were often operated as cooperatives, in livestock-intensive Indiana every farm had a silo for cattle and hog feed. Building those silos was a real craft; twenty feet across and sixty feet high, Brian and a helper could churn them out two a month. Indiana pigs and cows loved what came out of those silos, rich Indiana silage—the entire corn plant mashed up— that fed them all winter and into the spring. Seems, too, that they liked best what came out last, lush and slightly fermented silage from the bottom that nudged the livestock slightly drunk into May days.

No Indiana spring was complete either without the Barlows' eight-hour drive over to Waveland for Brian's birthday dinner at Grandmother McNutt's. April always meant morel gathering in Turkey Run Park. Brian and his troops would head out into the woods, gathering the largest morels and leaving the small ones for the return trip, knowing that within a few hours the little morels would double in size. That night there'd be a morel feast, with the mushrooms dipped in egg, then cracker crumbs, and cooked in butter, followed by Grandmother McNutt's chicken and noodles and a wild persimmon pudding for dessert (Edna McNutt kept wild persimmon purée in her freezer, ready to go year 'round). The next morning it was good-bye Waveland—wave when they come and wave when they go.

HOG HOLDER

Fresh Morels in Cracker Crumbs
and Butter

Grandmother McNutt's Chicken and Egg
Noodles with Rosemary

Buttered Broccoli or Green Salad

Stirred Wild Persimmon Pudding

———

Farm-raised produce, for the most part, tastes calm. Things that grow wild—mushrooms, berries, persimmons—often taste woodsy or smoky and slightly mysterious. Two of the following dishes use those wild flavors in a clear way. The delectable morels are coated with cracker crumbs to give a little crispness to the mushrooms when they are cooked; nothing else interferes. If you do not have fresh morels (and they are visible in certain good markets at certain times of the year), don't use dry ones, their delicacy has been lost; just make something else. In the persimmon pudding, the pungence of wild persimmons rises above the other spicy flavors. The tiny wild persimmons grow all over Indiana, but the familiar store-available variety of soft ripe persimmon—called "hachiya"—will give the pudding a perhaps less haunting but still fine flavor and texture. This persimmon dessert is different from steamed or baked puddings because it is stirred at frequent intervals. The extra effort is more than worth it.

Chicken and noodles is one of those dishes that, while plain, becomes grand when lovingly prepared. Made with a homemade stock and your own noodles and a sprinkling of fresh rosemary that helps the dish yearn for potatoes, it is one of the best reminders of farm life. Amazingly, if the bed of mashed potatoes on which it must be served is fluffy, and the noodles are well plumped in rich chicken broth, the dish is delicate and not overly starchy. Buttered broccoli or a salad is all I would serve on the side: Make it plain, make it good.

FRESH MORELS IN CRACKER CRUMBS AND BUTTER

■■

Serves 6

1½ pounds fresh morel mushrooms
3 eggs
Salt and freshly ground pepper to taste
2 cups fairly fine cracker crumbs, made from nonsweet
*   unflavored water-type crackers*
8 to 10 tablespoons butter

Trim the tips of the morel stems if they are tough or bruised; halve or quarter the mushrooms if they are very large (more than 2 or 3 ounces). Rinse the morels briefly in a large bowl of cold water, then place them in a sieve or colander to drain. Repeat with a fresh change of water if necessary (the morels may be soaked in salt water for a few minutes if they are very fresh and suspected of being buggy). Allow the mushrooms to drain thoroughly; pat them dry with a kitchen towel.

In a medium mixing bowl beat the eggs with a small amount of salt and pepper and 3 tablespoons water. Spread the cracker crumbs in a large pie plate. Drop the mushrooms, a few at a time, into the egg mixture, stirring to coat them well. Using a slotted spoon, lift the mushrooms out of the bowl and allow any excess egg mixture to drain. Stir and toss the morels in the crumbs until they are well coated, then place them on a large baking sheet; the mushrooms shouldn't wait more than 15 or 20 minutes before being cooked.

Melt 3 or 4 tablespoons butter in a large skillet set over medium-high heat. When the butter is hot, add as many mushrooms as the skillet can accommodate in one layer. Cook the morels until they are tender and nicely browned, for about 4 to 8 minutes, depending on the size of the mushrooms and the heat in the skillet. Lightly salt and pepper, place on a serving platter and keep warm while you cook the remaining mushrooms in additional melted butter. Serve on warm plates.

GRANDMOTHER MCNUTT'S CHICKEN AND EGG NOODLES WITH ROSEMARY

Serves 6

1 4½- to 5-pound fresh roasting chicken
2 medium carrots, scrubbed and chopped
2 stalks celery, rinsed and chopped
1 small onion, peeled and sliced
1 small leek, thoroughly washed and coarsely chopped
A few branches of fresh thyme, or 1 teaspoon dried thyme
    leaves
Small bunch of parsley
Salt and freshly ground pepper to taste
2 eggs
1⅓ cups unbleached all-purpose flour
2 teaspoons very finely chopped fresh rosemary

Cut up the chicken, setting aside the legs, thighs and breasts. Place the back, wings, neck and gizzard in a large pot with the aromatic vegetables, thyme and bunch of parsley. Cover with water and simmer for 45 minutes. Add the remaining pieces of chicken to the pot and continue simmering until the meat is just done: about 20 minutes for the breasts, 25 to 30 minutes for the dark meat. Remove the legs, thigh and breasts and set aside to cool. Strain the stock and remove all the fat. Pour the stock into a large saucepan; you should have about 2 to 2½ quarts. Season lightly with salt and pepper.

Using a wooden spoon or food processor, beat the eggs with the flour and ½ teaspoon salt, adding enough flour to make a slightly soft noodle dough (it should not be sticky). Place the dough on a lightly floured surface and knead for a minute or two. Divide in two. Roll out each half into a circle about 12 inches in diameter and about ¹⁄₁₆ inch thick; the dough will be elastic and require repeated strokes of the rolling pin (a pasta machine will also nicely accomplish the rolling out and, later on, the cutting of the noodle dough). Flour both sides of the dough generously and set aside for 20 minutes, turning over each round once so it dries evenly.

Remove the skin and bones from the chicken and pull apart the meat into large bite-size pieces. Season the meat lightly with salt and pepper.

Roll up each piece of noodle dough into a long cylinder and slice into noodles about ¼ inch wide. Unroll the noodles and lay on a baking sheet lined with a kitchen towel.

Bring the chicken stock to a simmer. Add the noodles and cook for about 15 minutes: They will swell and absorb much of the stock, and the flour clinging to them will thicken the gravy (they will be very soft, not *al dente*). Add the chicken pieces and simmer for another 5 minutes. Correct the seasoning with salt and pepper. Stir in the rosemary and serve the chicken and noodles over fluffy, buttery hot mashed potatoes. A green salad would be good on the side, or a little buttered broccoli.

STIRRED WILD PERSIMMON PUDDING

Serves 6 to 8

1¾ *cups unbleached all-purpose flour*
¾ *cup sugar*
½ *teaspoon cinnamon*
¼ *teaspoon allspice*
¼ *teaspoon nutmeg*
½ *teaspoon baking soda*
1 *cup milk*
1 *cup buttermilk*
1 *egg, beaten*
2 *tablespoons orange juice*

2 cups pulp of wild persimmon, or use the "domesticated"
  variety of soft persimmon (hachiya)
1 tablespoon butter, melted

Preheat the oven to 350° F.

Sift the dry ingredients into a mixing bowl. Combine the milk, buttermilk, egg and orange juice and stir into the flour mixture along with the persimmon purée and melted butter. Pour into a buttered 2-quart glass or porcelain baking dish and bake for 2½ hours, stirring around the sides and through the center of the pudding thoroughly every 15 minutes. Initially the pudding will increase slightly in volume, then gradually sink to a heavenly aromatic mud. The success of this pudding is in repeatedly "breaking" the set when you stir, which prolongs the baking time and allows the pudding to reduce to a delectable state. It is best served slightly hot, spooned onto plates and topped with slightly beaten cream with a little sugar and vanilla added.

14

LUTHERS

Springfield, Ohio

T hey make strong coffee in Berkeley, California, at least John Luther thinks so. Back in Springfield, Ohio, where John did most of his growing up, coffee was pretty pale stuff and something you drank with food—Midwest wine. But it wasn't just California coffee that gave John a jolt, it was also California's occasionally unsettling ease. Exempt for the first time from a German-Irish family of fourteen and grown and alone on the West Coast in 1986, John found himself unattached and a little uncertain. Fortunately there was another Luther nearby in San Leandro, a brother Jim in diesel engineering, who in John's first months away from Ohio gave him a home while John slipped into the ways of the West.

John is the son of Bob and Cese Luther who had twelve children: seven boys and five girls. They raised them in Fort Wayne, Indiana; briefly in Pleasanton, California, when Bob was transferred there with International Harvester; and finally in Springfield, Ohio. Growing up in a family so numerous was quite an experience. When the fourteen Luthers went to church they drove in two cars and filled an entire pew, and for Sunday dinner Cese—short for Cecilia—always made two roasts, one pork and one beef, to feed the long lines of Luthers at the table. In the Fort Wayne house there were bedrooms upstairs and bedrooms in the basement, three little Luthers to a room. With all those mouths to feed it's a good thing

Bob Luther was solid German. Stout and determined, he made a solid living. Cese Luther was stout and Irish, decisive on matters of discipline ("Shape up or I'll turn you over to your father") and disorganized around the house (John thinks she just gave up). The Luther kids actually preferred their mother's let's-get-it-over-with kind of discipline to the plodding authority of their dad, and would take a sharp scold or a smack from their mom any day to Bob's probing tactics which, rather horribly, urged them to reason. Who wanted to sit in a think-tank with Papa when you could be out revving up your roller skates? There wasn't that much judicial activity around the Luther household anyway; as John remembers it, misbehavior and the Midwest were usually strangers. Jello, now, was another matter.

Jello and the Midwest were not strangers. Those cheery heartland aspics were nearly as much a part of the Ohio-to-Iowa landscape as corn itself. Jello was honest, unbesmirched by butterfat, and it refreshed Midwest tables laden with beige food (corn, macaroni, pork, and so on). Jello also traveled well, to casserole suppers and church socials, not to mention other sudden destinations. As local legend had it, any dessert that could survive a detour off a county road through a ditch and land intact, still on its owner's lap, in a vehicle resting on its side in a pasture and then proceed on schedule in a follow car and show up in the headlines the next morning— any dessert that sturdy was worthy of a place of honor on Ohio tables. John Luther remembers Jello appearing at large family parties especially around the holidays. Jello was something you could dress up—layer or mold and flavor with fruit—and yet it remained a basic food. And given the feat of just getting food for fourteen onto the table, sticking to basics was a good idea. As a boy John liked those basics. His favorite birthday dinner (Cese maintained a repertoire of twelve birthday dinners, one for each kid) was pork roast with potatoes and carrots, dinner rolls, plenty of iceberg with buttermilk dressing and (in place of Jello) his mom's fragrant German chocolate cake, one of the few desserts she made from scratch. For other birthdays Cese usually made standard white cake, but not for her boy John.

In his third year of high school John made a breakthrough.

Looking for an easy "A," John and some of his cronies, including a couple of jocks, signed up for a course that in the sixties would have been a sissy class but in the seventies was a status class. They signed up for Gourmet Cooking I, and what for John started out as a lark became a fascination. True, John was only bridging the fundamentals of two distant cultures, Ohio and France; but journeying from chicken noodle soup to *soupe à l'oignon gratinée*, from pot roast to *boeuf bourguignon*, was one giant step for a docile, red-haired kid in Springfield. Eventually John's curiosity about food led to assertiveness: Appearing after school in Cese's kitchen, he'd stick his finger in the dinner-in-progress and, with green-eyed calm, make suggestions. A few dried herbs here, a little red wine there (John first had to make sure there *was* a little red wine in the house), maybe even a little butter—and the Luther supper was transformed. Cese was thrilled. Cooking all those years for all those Luthers, she was just worn out. John's dad, somewhat worn out himself from a lifetime of clean-cut cooking, welcomed the change as Luther food shifted slightly away from casserole gothic.

With Gourmet Cooking I under his belt, John had his juices going. On his weekend job at Baskin-Robbins he started tinkering with desserts, poking through the corporate cookbook on becalmed winter afternoons and putting together ice cream cakes. Later on, after two standard years of business classes at standard Ohio U. in Athens, John decided he was not bullish on business and, enrolling himself in an apprenticeship culinary program in Columbus, returned to his first love.

Like other fledgling cooks through the ages, John was drawn into the absorbing rite of apprenticeship. Working with a young Ohio chef, Kent Rigsby, who was fresh from a kiwi-laden sojourn in California's evolving new-style restaurants, John extracted plenty from his first restaurant experience. While partially subscribing to the slavish novelties emanating from California and France, Kent also had the good sense to reveal the discipline and value of classic flavors and techniques to his apprentice cooks, and it was the classic, especially, that John absorbed.

In 1985, after two years in apprenticeship, John began to sense that Ohio had taught him all it could teach about cooking. Murmurings from California, most persistently from Berkeley, beckoned him with their emphasis on cottage industry and the integrity of ingredients that recalled rural culinary traditions. Feeling marginally rural himself and needing to grow, John embarked for the West and quickly learned the second rule of culinary education (the first being the necessity of apprenticeship): that cooks get jobs anywhere they go. John started in at the Buttercup Bakery, baking handmade pies and his mother's definitive German chocolate cake. After four months of *that*, word reached him: Alice wants you. Alice being, natcherly, Alice Waters of the restaurant Chez Panisse. And so it was that a young Ohio man raised on tuna casserole found his way into one of the most contemplated kitchens in the solar system. While working his pasta/lettuce shift—four hours of pasta-making followed by four hours of lettuce leaf scrutiny—John marked his passage into the realm of buckwheat-pasta-with-chard.

It's quite a journey from Bob and Cese's place to Alice's. But John is a good traveler. He's thinking about France next. Why not? There must be a few French kitchens ready for a suggestion or two from old green eyes.

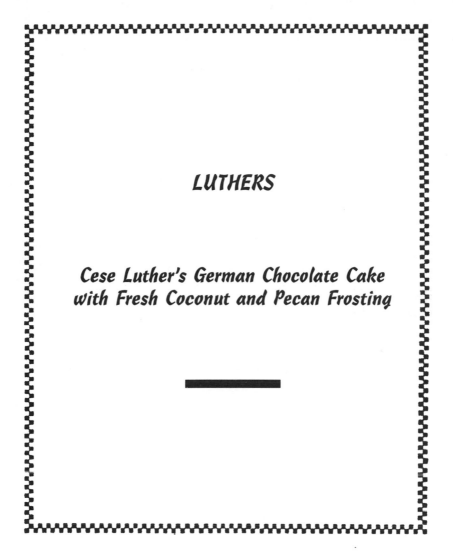

LUTHERS

Cese Luther's German Chocolate Cake with Fresh Coconut and Pecan Frosting

Cese Luther's German chocolate cake is a grand American layer cake. It is fluffy, fragrant with vanilla and coconut, and it has a gentle chocolate flavor. Use fresh coconut if you can; its clear, milky, barely sweet flavor, and its crunchiness make it worth the extra work. But the cake is excellent even made with a good-quality packaged coconut (the best source is a health food store).

CESE LUTHER'S GERMAN CHOCOLATE CAKE WITH FRESH COCONUT AND PECAN FROSTING

A 3-layer, 9-inch cake for 12 to 14

4 ounces (German) sweet chocolate, broken into small pieces
½ cup boiling water
1 cup unsalted butter at room temperature
2 cups sugar
4 eggs, separated
1 teaspoon vanilla extract
2½ cups cake flour
1 teaspoon baking soda
½ teaspoon salt
1 cup liquid—fresh coconut juice reserved from 1 whole
   coconut used in the frosting recipe (usually 3 to 4
   tablespoons) plus buttermilk OR 1 cup buttermilk if you
   are using packaged coconut
½ teaspoon cream of tartar

Preheat the oven to 350° F.

Place the chocolate in a small bowl and add the boiling water; stir occasionally until the chocolate is melted and smooth. In a separate bowl cream the butter and gradually add the sugar, beating until the mixture is fluffy. Beat in the egg yolks and the vanilla, then the chocolate. Sift together the dry ingredients and add alternately with the liquid to the chocolate mixture. Beat the egg whites with a pinch of salt and the cream of tartar until they are just stiff; stir a large spoonful of the whites into the batter, then fold in the remaining whites. Pour into 3 buttered and dusted-with-flour 9-inch cake pans. Bake for 30 to 40 minutes, until the layers have begun to pull away from the sides of the pans and a toothpick inserted in the center comes out clean. Cool for 20 minutes in the pans, then unmold the layers on racks to finish cooling.

COCONUT PECAN FROSTING

1 cup evaporated milk
1 cup sugar
3 egg yolks
½ cup butter, cut into pieces
1 teaspoon vanilla extract
1 whole fresh coconut (or 1⅓ cups shredded packaged coconut,
  preferably unsweetened)
1 cup chopped pecans
Powdered sugar (optional)

Combine the evaporated milk, sugar, egg yolks, butter and vanilla in a heavy-bottomed saucepan and cook over medium-low heat, stirring constantly, until the mixture thickens, for about 10 to 12 minutes. Do not boil. Remove from the heat and stir briefly to cool.

If you are using a fresh coconut, pierce the eyes with an ice pick and drain out the juice (reserve and use in the cake recipe). Place the coconut in a 350° F. oven for about 20 minutes; cool for a few moments (baking the coconut briefly facilitates the removal of the coconut meat). Wrap the coconut in a kitchen towel to keep the shell from flying all over the place, and whack it hard several times with a hammer to crack it open. Pry the coconut away from the shell, using a sturdy implement such as an oyster knife or a clean screwdriver but *not* a knife (a thin blade could snap). Using a small paring knife, peel the brown papery skin off the coconut meat. Grate the coconut in a food processor or in small batches in a blender. Fold the fresh or packaged coconut into the frosting along with the chopped pecans.

When the layers are cool, spread the coconut pecan frosting over them as you stack them on top of each other, leaving the sides plain. Dust the sides with powdered sugar if you wish. The cake is best served at room temperature.

15

···

PICKER BUSHES

Royal Oak, Michigan

J eannette Costeiu lives among coconut palms now, but she grew up after World War II under the elms and oaks of the northern Detroit suburbs, a skinny brown-haired tomboy. Jeannette was the youngest of three daughters in the Costeiu family, and with no boys around, her father John treated Jeannette as his son. It was a role she loved, puttering around cars with her father and handing him his tools when his head was stuck under the chassis or hood, or zooming in the dead of winter onto frozen Lake Michigan in John's pride and joy, a home-restored 1934 Cadillac La Salle, to go fishing for smelts. John taught Jeannette his love of the outdoors and also of mechanical stuff, and it made father and daughter inseparable. Jeannette had been drawn to her dad from the moment her new green eyes looked into his deep warm blue ones. As Jeannette or anyone else could see, John Costeiu was a magnificent man, and his winning smile and sense of adventure were what propelled him and his family through life.

The Costeius were Romanian. John Costeiu had left his troubled country in the 1930's and met his wife Valeria in the United States while she was also visiting from Romania. The couple returned to their homeland just long enough to collect their belongings and marry: The States was it for them. John bought a farm outside of Detroit as a gift to his bride and they raised their three daughters on it, as well as Guernseys, Jerseys, Holsteins, chickens, lambs and two goats. On that farm the Costeius had a smokehouse nicknamed "the bomb shelter" where they made hams. There were apple, peach and pear orchards, black walnut trees and haystacks. That's where Valeria learned to drive, careening around those haystacks. While Valeria was practicing her double-clutching, John would often hoist two-year-old Jeannette up into the hayloft and deposit her next to him while he worked pitching hay down. Jeannette had to sit perfectly still near the busy hayfork or she would have been pitched down too. Neither father nor daughter ever flinched; that silent trust, begun in a hayloft, lasted until his death.

In the late 1940's when Jeannette was six, John began to sense that prosperity might lie closer to the city, so he sold his farm and moved his family to Royal Oak on the outskirts of Detroit, where he bought a grocery store, the Highway Market. Like most immigrant shopkeepers John and Valeria Costeiu worked long hours with no complaints. They were prospering, that's what counted. So most nights around the Costeiu house the children fed themselves. Jeannette and her older sisters Virginia and Helen, who had finished high school and worked during the day at the store, usually had a noon meal together with their parents. Valeria cooked wholesome stews with dumplings and served them to her girls in the stockroom at the back of the store. After lunch Jeannette would be shepherded back to school a couple of miles down the road. Then at night Jeannette returned home with her sisters and sat down to a good soup of their own making, keeping it warm for their parents who arrived late to find their daughters already quiet in their beds.

But on Christmas Eve it was different. During the last week of extra-long hours at the store Valeria made time to begin preparations for the family's Christmas dinner, working in the store kitchen stuffing fennel sausages, grinding fresh pork and veal for the turkey stuffing, and at the very last, steaming and puréeing pumpkin, and peeling, coring and slicing crisp Michigan Jonathan apples for the pies. By the afternoon before Christmas the Highway Market was sold out and the Closed sign went up early. John's work was still not done, though. He always worked late on Christmas Eve, completing his last essential task of the season: the filling of thirty or

so Christmas baskets for the needy. The tasty items—some slices
of ham or a dozen fresh sausages, perhaps some of Valeria's delicate
kefli cookies stuffed with walnuts, some shiny McIntosh apples—
were chosen and wrapped with care. John wanted to share his
prosperity with others.

On Christmas Eve in 1953, while John worked late, Valeria was
home early to have supper with her daughters and put her kitchen
in order for Christmas day. Pie dough was rolled and fitted into
pans and pinched, poppyseed strudel were wrapped and brushed
with butter and put to bake. Then there was supper of string bean
soup, crisp ham slices and potato salad, easy food on a busy night
eaten in the warm kitchen.

The sisters were happy to have their mother at home. Like min-
nows they drifted between her and the Christmas tree, the two
centers of attention in the house. By eleven John entered into the
bright scene and enjoyed a good late supper before it was time for
the family to pull on their heavy coats, pile into the prized La Salle
and glide off to midnight mass at the Romanian Orthodox Church
down on Seven Mile Road in Detroit. During the mass the smoky
perfumes and gilded hush of the orthodox church gathered Jeannette
into the arms of the night, and finally of half-sleep. Well after one
in the morning, while Helen and Virginia moved drowsily to the
car, Jeannette rested peacefully in her father's arms as he carried his
"little chicken" out of the church for the drive home. The weightless
warmth of her Aunt Livia's hand-stuffed goose down comforter
floating over her in bed was Jeannette's last impression of that
Christmas Eve of her tenth year. By the time the rise and drift of
her parents' voices finally expired and the house joined the steady
silence of the Christmas snowfall, Jeannette was in too deep a sleep
to know it.

That Christmas in the early fifties was special for the Costeiu
family in many ways. Sure, there were Santa Claus's muddy footprints across the living room rug just like every year (John got those
footprints perfect several nights before Christmas—since there was
no time on Christmas Eve—then the rug was turned over to hide
the evidence until Christmas morning). And the holiday feast took
place as it always did at one o'clock in the afternoon, which allowed

plenty of time for appetites to revive for the ritual seven o'clock supper of leftovers. There were the familiar blessings and toasts with John's homemade red wine. And, as always, it was just John and Valeria and their brood, with perhaps an aunt or uncle or two. Jeannette and her sisters grew up not knowing their grandparents, who had never made it out of the old country, and their absence had helped draw the Costeiu family even closer together.

So what set that Christmas apart from other Costeiu Christmases? Two things. First, the electric train that was waiting under the tree for Jeannette that Christmas morning and widened her already full eyes. It told Jeannette what she had always yearned to know: that she was as good as any boy. That gift of respect from her father was the most cherished possession of Jeannette's childhood.

And second? It was the last Christmas the Costeius were to spend as a real family. Jeannette's sisters were nearly grown and before another year had passed they both would advance to new jobs and to sweethearts and eventual marriages. The Christmas of 1953 at 527 South Stevenson was a Christmas of closeness. The family changed after then.

The wiry ruffian of Royal Oak—who preferred to beat boys at baseball rather than kiss 'em, and who, if anyone tried a kiss anyway, gave him a punch and tossed him into the fearsome "picker bushes" that roamed the fields of Jeannette's youth—grew to be a woman of radiance. And she still leaves the boys in the dust. Sure, she's had sweethearts, but no one was her match. Besides, who could match her dad? He was her hero. The people of Royal Oak must have felt the same; when John Costeiu died in 1976 half the town came out for his funeral. After that Jeannette moved to Florida, where she leads the charmed life of a southern place. But her past is with her: the rich blood of Romania that shaped her face, the loyalty and generosity of immigrant family life in a Michigan suburb that shaped her heart.

PICKER BUSHES

String Bean Soup

Crisp Ham Slices in Red Wine

Potato Salad with Fresh Dill

Kefli (Horn Cookies with Walnuts)

Warm Cranberry Compote

———

This menu from the Costeiu family makes a good winter supper. The crisp ham slices are an appealing alternative to cold ham, and the simple red wine reduction adds some extra flavor. Valeria's potato salad, made with olive oil, vinegar and *lots* of fresh dill (fresh Michigan dill is one of the joys of that state and it seems to go on year 'round) is lighter than usual potato salads made with mayonnaise, and yet it is substantial enough, along with the string bean soup, to round out the meal. That soup is the simplest kind, having only the flavor of the beans, a little leek, olive oil and thyme. Increasingly I find a meat or poultry stock in a soup to be unnecessary. It seems to muddy the clear flavor of whatever vegetable is used. Water-based soups are wonderful if you have good vegetables and good herbs, and the good sense not to add much else.

Romanian *kefli* are delicate cookies, really small pastries stuffed with homemade walnut paste, that melt in your mouth when eaten recently out of the oven. *Kefli* really need no accompaniment, although at the Costeiu house there would have been home-dried Michigan prunes stewed with lemon and vanilla. I have included another fruit compote as a possible accompaniment, one made with cranberries that are stewed in a rich caramel, then finished with a little bourbon and mint.

STRING BEAN SOUP

Serves 6

1 *medium leek, trimmed of the stem and any ragged or dirty green leaves*
3 *tablespoons olive oil plus 2 tablespoons (optional)*
1¼ *pounds green beans, washed and strings and stems removed*

Salt and freshly ground pepper to taste
1½ teaspoons fresh thyme leaves, or ½ teaspoon dried thyme
*   leaves*
¼ cup grated good Parmesan cheese

Cut deep slits into the green part of the leek and wash the leek thoroughly under running cold water. Chop it coarsely. Warm the 3 tablespoons olive oil in a large saucepan set over medium-low heat, add the chopped leek and stir briefly to coat with the oil. Cover, and cook the leek for 4 or 5 minutes, stirring occasionally. Uncover, add 1½ quarts water to the pan, and bring to the boil. Add the green beans and 2 teaspoons salt and boil rapidly until the beans are very tender, for 8 to 10 minutes or more, depending on the kind and size of the beans. Stir in the thyme leaves. Purée the soup briefly in a blender (the soup is good when not perfectly smooth), or put it through the medium disk of a food mill. Correct the seasoning with salt and pepper, and add the remaining 2 table-spoons olive oil if you wish. Serve hot in warmed soup bowls or plates and sprinkle with the Parmesan cheese.

CRISP HAM SLICES IN RED WINE

Serves 6

6 tablespoons olive oil
6 baked ham slices, about ⅓ inch thick, at room temperature
½ cup finely chopped onion
Salt and freshly ground pepper to taste
1½ cups good red wine (a Pinot Noir or a Zinfandel)

Set 2 large skillets over high heat and add 2 tablespoons olive oil to each pan. When the oil is hot, add as many of the ham slices as will comfortably fit in the pans; don't crowd them. Sear for about 2 minutes on one side, pressing on the meat so that the slices brown evenly. Turn the slices and sear for about 1 minute. Remove to a platter and keep warm while you brown the rest of the ham.

Add the remaining 2 tablespoons olive oil to one of the skillets set over medium-low heat. Add the onion, salt and pepper lightly and stir to coat the onions with the oil. Cover and cook for 4 or 5 minutes, stirring occasionally. Uncover, add the wine and boil down rapidly over high heat, until there is about ½ cup liquid in the pan. Scrape the sides and bottom of the skillet to dissolve any of the caramelized meat juices. Correct the seasoning with salt and pepper. Pour the sauce over the ham slices, add some freshly ground pepper and serve.

POTATO SALAD WITH FRESH DILL

Serves 6

3 pounds boiling potatoes, washed
Salt and freshly ground pepper to taste
2 to 3 tablespoons white wine vinegar
½ cup olive oil
9 or 10 thin round slices of peeled red onion
3 tablespoons chopped fresh dill
1 tablespoon chopped parsley

Boil the potatoes in lightly salted water until tender; drain and set aside to cool. Peel the potatoes, cut into ¼-inch slices and, while still warm, toss them gently in a mixing bowl with salt and pepper, the vinegar and olive oil. Place the potatoes on a serving platter. Toss the onion slices with a little olive oil and vinegar and arrange them over the potatoes. Sprinkle the dill and parsley over all. The salad is best served at room temperature.

KEFLI (Horn Cookies with Walnuts)

∎∎

About 3o cookies

2 cups unbleached all-purpose flour
1 cup butter at room temperature
8 ounces cream cheese, softened
1 tablespoon vanilla extract
1 teaspoon grated lemon rind
2½ cups walnuts
¾ cup sugar
3 egg whites
¼ teaspoon salt
2 tablespoons apple jelly
1 egg yolk lightly beaten with 2 teaspoons water
Powdered sugar in a shaker

Blend together the flour, butter, cream cheese, 1 teaspoon of the vanilla and lemon rind either in a food processor or with a mixer. Shape the dough into balls about the size of a large walnut, dust them with flour and set them on a baking sheet. Cover with plastic wrap and refrigerate for at least an hour.

In a food processor (or in 2 or 3 batches in a blender) pulverize the walnuts with the sugar, then place in a mixing bowl. Beat the egg whites with the salt until they form fairly stiff peaks; fold them into the walnut powder along with the remaining 2 teaspoons vanilla and the apple jelly. The filling will be a sticky paste.

Preheat the oven to 325° F.

Roll out the balls of dough 2 or 3 at a time (keep the remaining dough chilled while you work) on a lightly floured surface into rounds about 4 inches in diameter. The rounds should be about ⅛ inch thick. Place about 2 teaspoons of the walnut filling in the center of each round, roll the dough up like a cigar, enclosing the filling with the dough. Fold the two ends of dough in toward each other to form crescent-shaped cookies. Place the *kefli* on a lightly buttered baking sheet, brush gently with the egg yolk glaze and bake for about 25 minutes, until the cookies are very lightly browned. Cool on a rack, then dust lightly with the powdered sugar. These cookies are deliciously flaky and at their best when served warm. They can be made 2 or 3 days in advance and stored when cool in an airtight container or on a platter covered with plastic wrap; rewarm the *kefli* in a moderate oven for 5 or 6 minutes before serving. Add a fresh dusting of powdered sugar if you wish.

WARM CRANBERRY COMPOTE

Serves 6

5 tablespoons butter
¾ cup sugar
3 cups fresh cranberries, picked over
¾ cup fresh orange juice
½ teaspoon vanilla extract, or a 1-inch piece of vanilla bean,
*   split in half*
Pinch of salt
1 to 2 tablespoons bourbon
1 teaspoon chopped fresh mint

Melt the butter in a large heavy-bottomed saucepan, add the sugar and cook over high heat until the sugar has caramelized to a rich brown. The sugar will liquefy and turn clear just before it begins to caramelize; watch closely at that point that it doesn't burn. Off the heat add the cranberries, watching out for splatters from the hot caramel, and the orange juice. Return the pan to medium heat and stir for several minutes, scraping the bottom, until the caramel has completely dissolved. Add the vanilla and pinch of salt and simmer the cranberries until they are very soft and have thickened slightly, for about 15 to 20 minutes. Remove the vanilla bean if you have used it. Off the heat add the bourbon and mint. As it is rather richly flavored, serve small portions of the compote which is best served warm.

Note: This compote, which freezes very well, is also very good made in the summer with fresh red plums.

16

DAVE AND LARRY

Davenport, Iowa

Davenport, Iowa, is near the only section of the Mississippi that runs east to west, instead of north to south like most self-respecting stretches of the River. Apart from that, there's not much startling about Davenport. Roger and Loretta Beckwith, both German descendants and offspring of native Iowans, settled there on West 8th Street in the late 1950's and felt right at home.

The Beckwith house was one of many similar houses in central Davenport, all two-storied and white, all with porch swings, and all within walking distance of church, Ray Eklund's butcher shop or the corner German bakery. Neighborhood shops were especially pivotal to the German housewives of Davenport who shopped and cooked every day ("stocking up for the week" had not yet got a grip on the town's resolute cooks).

For Duff and Larry, as Roger and Loretta—high school sweethearts—were always known, raising a family of eight was a substantial undertaking. Actually Duff had it easy, all he had to do was report for duty to the phone company and come home to an evening of ease and a good dinner. But Larry, who worked full-time for twenty-six years as a Tupperware manager, trudged home at the end of the day having converted her quota of Tupperware users only to face another clamoring bunch, hungry not for food-storage gospel, but for grub.

David Beckwith remembers his mom's kitchen as a mess. If you call big and busy a mess, then it was. Larry's kitchen had a huge table surrounded by benches along the back wall. On benches, David recalls, you could station "more small butts on less wood" than on chairs. And the room served endless purposes. It was used for breakfast, then packing Tupperware, then lunch if anyone was there (with eight kids someone usually was), then after-school snacks, then dinner, then for homework. The kitchen was a busy place. And it evolved that, on days when Larry had a lot of Tupperware to distribute, ten-year-old David would take over some of the cooking. Larry, who was a good simple cook, taught David some of the basics such as chili. Then he advanced to pot roast, which for the Beckwiths, situated in the Midwest casserole belt as they were, filled a family need: Get it in the oven and you're done. So little blond David, although not the oldest—his brother Steven was but he was also a jock so that ruled him out for any usefulness in the cooking department—David became his mother's second-in-command in the kitchen and so unknowingly began his first phase of apprenticeship.

Growing up in Davenport was kind of wonderfully regular. Walking home under the elm trees from St. Joseph's Catholic school, David had favorite stops. One was at the potato chip factory where for 10¢ you could get a bag full to the brim with freshly made potato chips, and for another 15¢ you got a bottle of pop from the crotchety old lady who ran the counter. But David didn't stroll out the door to munch and sip his way home without first lingering to watch the potato chips riding around on conveyor belts before they made their way into a bag and eventually into his mouth. Once back home and out of his school clothes, David liked to poke around his dad's backyard where all kinds of good things were growing—beans, squash, pumpkins, strawberries, tomatoes and, of course, corn. The tomatoes in Duff's garden grew to be the size of softballs and they showed David life among the seasons: Not only was a succulent, ripe, out-of-the-garden tomato out of this world, there was also a kind of contentment in the wait for the season. Sprawled under the buckeye trees near the dozing garden, David inhaled the scents of plenty.

When David started high school he also started his first after-school job at Eklund's Butcher Shop, where he worked for five years, first as a stock boy, then as a meat-cutter and sausage-maker. David liked hanging out in the butcher shop; being around voluminous food preparation felt natural to him. He also got a kick out of watching Ray Eklund squirm when Larry Beckwith strode in to buy her pot roast or some pork chops. David's mom was wise to butcher's thumbs that wandered onto the scale to embellish a sale. So when Mr. Eklund hoisted the Beckwith daily ration onto the scale it was often with a wince provoked by Larry Beckwith's bark to keep his heavy thumbs to himself. David, lurking in the background, would snicker into his sausages and then look scrupulously busy when old man Eklund glared in his direction. David didn't mind: At Eklund's you got a crash course in cautionary tales as well as in butchery.

The food that David grew up around was influenced by neither fashion nor leisure: Iowa food was for people who worked hard. Everyday food was plain and wholesome, and dessert was usually reserved to dress up Sunday dinner. David's grandmother, who lived a few blocks away and whom everyone called Aunt Betty, was the baker in the family and quite a baker she was. She turned out mean pies, German chocolate cakes of course, and scrumptious frosted chocolate cookies the size of butter plates. David's favorite dessert was chocolate cake or cookies, homemade vanilla ice cream and strawberries out of the garden. Aunt Betty hand-cranked her ice cream, usually only on birthdays, but it wasn't the work that relegated ice cream to special occasions, it was the cost of ingredients. Cream was expensive and required a special order with the milkman. On days when David saw that extra cream-flap up on the front porch when he headed off to school his step always became a little jauntier.

As time went by and David's kinship with cooking and eating grew, Larry Beckwith eventually started saying her son would have a restaurant one day. And Larry was right. David did end up with a restaurant. Not called Dave's, like she thought, and not for that matter on the Wapsui River in eastern Iowa, where the Beckwith men went on weekends to fish catfish and drink beer. Still, spitting distance from the Pacific Ocean is no slouch, and if you stop some night at the Central 159 in Monterey and look around, you may find David Beckwith snickering into his sausages and tossing traces of Iowa into the straight-ahead Davidfood he sends out to his customers who sit, many of them, on fancy benches.

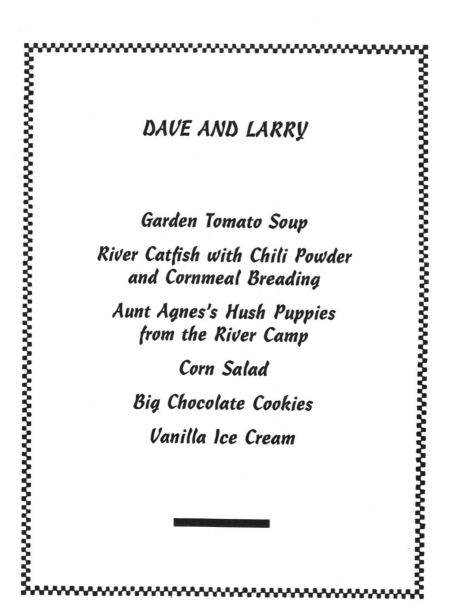

DAVE AND LARRY

Garden Tomato Soup

River Catfish with Chili Powder
and Cornmeal Breading

Aunt Agnes's Hush Puppies
from the River Camp

Corn Salad

Big Chocolate Cookies

Vanilla Ice Cream

Catfish fries on the Wapsui—short for Wapsuipinican—River were a cherished Beckwith clan ritual. On summer Friday evenings the Beckwith men would depart to spend the weekend being males in the wild—fishing and swigging beer—at Aunt Agnes's river camp. On Sunday the Beckwith women, including Aunt Agnes, arrived on the premises for the fish fry. Fried catfish and hush puppies generally went together. Why and how is a tale in itself. At rural catfish fries in the Midwest and in the South, at the end of the day the dogs would gather around the fire with their masters and whine and eye the frying fish. To hush them up the fish-fryer would mix together the leftover cornmeal-and-flour and milk-and-egg mixtures used for breading the fish, and drop it into the remaining hot fat to make dumplings for the dogs. Hence hush puppies. Which is all news to me.

Real river catfish have a rich, gamy flavor—David calls it gritty—which is smoothed over somewhat by a spicy, rough cornmeal breading. David's hush puppies too are enhanced with garlic and fresh thyme. The tomato soup, on the other hand, is gentle with the flavors of aromatic vegetables simmered with a little apple and pear (for sweetness and a slight tang). With really wonderful garden tomatoes, you could probably consider the fruit optional. Red peppers and olive oil, and shallots and white wine add extra flavors to the corn salad to make it a little bit gentrified.

We have Aunt Betty's best friend Pauline to thank for Aunt Betty's chocolate cookie recipe. Aunt Betty is no longer with us in this life, but Pauline, who is in her nineties, used to bake the same chocolate cookies and dredged up the recipe. Pauline actually called them devil's food cookies, as they are on the cakey side. The accompanying vanilla ice cream is deeply flavored with both vanilla bean and vanilla extract. The slight amount of honey, and drops of optional rum, don't really add other flavors, they just make the vanilla more so.

GARDEN TOMATO SOUP

Serves 6 to 8

2 tablespoons olive oil
2 stalks celery, rinsed and chopped
1 white onion, peeled and chopped
2 medium carrots, peeled and chopped
1 medium leek, trimmed, cleaned and chopped
1 cup dry white wine
3 pounds ripe tomatoes, cores removed and chopped
1 green apple, peeled, cored and chopped
1 ripe pear, peeled, cored and chopped
1 quart tomato juice, homemade or good-quality bottled juice
Salt and freshly ground pepper to taste
¼ teaspoon cayenne
1 cup half-and-half

In a large pot heat the olive oil, then stir in the celery, onion, carrots and leek and cook over medium heat, stirring occasionally, for about 10 minutes. Add the white wine and simmer for 1 minute. Add the tomatoes, apple, pear and the tomato juice and simmer for 20 minutes. Season the soup with salt and pepper and the cayenne. Stir in the half-and-half and simmer another 20 minutes. Either purée the soup in a blender, or if you have cut things into a nice size serve the soup directly from the pot.

RIVER CATFISH WITH CHILI POWDER AND CORNMEAL BREADING

Serves 6

2 cups yellow cornmeal
1 cup all-purpose flour
1 teaspoon salt
1 teaspoon freshly ground black pepper
½ teaspoon cayenne
¼ cup dark chili powder
¼ cup light chili powder
2 cups buttermilk
1 whole egg, beaten
3 pounds fresh river catfish fillets (or farm-raised catfish is
     okay)
⅓ cup olive or peanut oil
Wedges of lemon

Place the dry ingredients in a mixing bowl and sift together with your hands. Combine the buttermilk and egg in a shallow pan. Season the fish fillets lightly.

In one or two large cast-iron skillets heat the oil until it pops when sprinkled with a few drops of cold water. Dip each catfish fillet into the buttermilk and egg batter, then dredge it in the cornmeal mixture. Cook the fish in the hot oil for 3 or 4 minutes on one side, then turn and lower the heat, giving the catfish another 1 or 2 minutes in the pan. Remove from the pan. If you wish, drain the fillets on absorbent paper. Serve with the lemon wedges.

AUNT AGNES'S HUSH PUPPIES FROM THE RIVER CAMP

Serves 6 to 8

3 cups yellow cornmeal
3 cups unbleached all-purpose flour
1 cup masa harina *(fine corn flour)*
3 tablespoons baking powder
2 teaspoons cayenne
1½ teaspoons salt
1 tablespoon freshly ground black pepper
2 teaspoons white pepper
1 tablespoon chopped fresh thyme leaves, or 2 teaspoons dried thyme leaves
1 bunch of green onions, finely chopped
8 garlic cloves, peeled and finely chopped
6 eggs
3 cups milk
6 tablespoons butter, melted
Peanut oil for frying

Combine the dry ingredients in a mixing bowl with the thyme, onions and garlic. Beat together the liquid ingredients and with as few stirs as possible combine with the dry mixture. Heat the oil in a large cast-iron skillet to about 375° F. and carefully drop in the batter by tablespoonfuls. The oil should come about two-thirds of the way up the side of the batter balls. Cook approximately 5 minutes, turning the balls occasionally, or until golden brown and springy to the touch. Drain on paper towels and keep warm while you continue frying hush puppies until all of the batter is used up. Serve with the catfish.

CORN SALAD

....

Serves 6

¼ *cup olive oil*
3 *large shallots, peeled*
2 *red bell peppers, halved, cored, seeded and cut into strips*
Salt and freshly ground pepper to taste
4 *cups fresh uncooked corn cut off the cob (about 5 or 6 ears)*
1 *garlic clove, peeled and minced*
½ *teaspoon fresh thyme leaves, or* ¼ *teaspoon dried thyme leaves*
½ *teaspoon cracked black peppercorns*
1½ *teaspoons coarsely chopped parsley*
3 *tablespoons dry white wine*
2 *teaspoons sherry vinegar or red wine vinegar*

Heat 2 tablespoons of the olive oil in a large skillet, add the shallots and cook, stirring constantly, over low heat until almost tender, for about 5 minutes. Remove the shallots from the pan. Pour in the remaining oil, add the red peppers and season lightly with salt and pepper. Cook over medium-low heat, stirring occasionally, for about 10 minutes, until the peppers are just tender. Using a slotted spoon, remove the peppers from the pan and combine in a mixing bowl with the shallots. Add the corn and garlic to the skillet and cook, stirring, until the corn is quite tender, about 6 minutes. Using the slotted spoon, transfer the corn from the pan to the bowl with the red peppers and shallots, and stir in the thyme, cracked black pepper, parsley, white wine and vinegar. Correct the seasoning with salt and pepper. Serve warm or at room temperature.

BIG CHOCOLATE COOKIES

■■■

For 12 to 15 cookies

5 tablespoons unsweetened cocoa powder
2 cups unbleached all-purpose flour
½ teaspoon baking soda
½ teaspoon salt
1 tablespoon baking powder
½ cup sugar
1 stick unsalted butter
½ cup milk
½ cup buttermilk
Chocolate Frosting (recipe follows)

Preheat the oven to 400° F.

Stir together the dry ingredients. Cut in the butter until pea-sized granules form. Stir in the milk and buttermilk as quickly as possible. Chill the dough for 1 hour, then roll out ½ inch thick on a well-floured board, flouring the dough as you work, and cut out rounds about 4 inches in diameter. Reassemble the scraps of dough and roll and cut out cookies again. Any final scraps can be squished together and baked along with the cookies (or eat them raw). Bake the cookies on lightly greased baking sheets for 10 to 12 minutes. They should be springy, and mostly dry when pierced with a broom straw or small knife. Remove to a rack; frost when cool.

Note: This recipe makes a soft and slightly sticky dough. If you find it tricky to handle, simply scoop ¼-cup amounts of dough onto the baking sheet and flatten them gently with floured fingers.

CHOCOLATE FROSTING

2 tablespoons unsalted butter
3 ounces unsweetened chocolate
3 tablespoons hot water or milk
⅛ teaspoon salt
2 cups (about) sifted powdered sugar
1 teaspoon vanilla extract

Melt the butter and chocolate together. Stir in the hot water or milk, salt, powdered sugar and vanilla (adjust the amount of powdered sugar to achieve the desired consistency). Cool, then spread over the chocolate cookies.

VANILLA ICE CREAM

About 2 quarts

3 cups milk
2 cups heavy cream
1 vanilla bean, split in half
1 tablespoon vanilla extract
1 tablespoon honey
1 tablespoon dark rum (optional)
2 eggs and 2 extra yolks
¾ cup sugar
Pinch of salt
*Strawberries from the garden, washed, stemmed and sliced, if
    you have them*

In a large heavy-bottomed saucepan scald the milk and cream with the vanilla bean, vanilla extract, honey and optional rum. In a mixing bowl beat together the eggs and yolks, then gradually add the sugar and pinch of salt, beating until the mixture is pale and slightly thick. Beat in the hot milk mixture, very slowly at first and then more rapidly as the eggs warm through. Return the mixture to the saucepan and stir constantly over medium heat until the custard thickens slightly, enough to coat a wooden spoon with a light layer (near a simmer but nowhere near a boil; a good test is to watch the foam on the surface, which disappears when the custard begins to thicken). If the custard overheats and bits of the egg curdle, simply smooth it out in the blender. Immediately remove the pan from the heat, pour the custard into a bowl and continue stirring for 1 or 2 minutes. Set aside to cool; do not cover. When room temperature, remove the vanilla bean, scraping the sticky contents of the bean into the custard. Churn the custard in an ice cream maker.

Serve in bowls with the big chocolate cookies on the side, and, if you have them, very ripe strawberries from the garden.

17

....

BAKING FOR
HER LIFE

Huot, Minnesota

Her first winter in Crookston, Minnesota, Hallie Harron
went in the ditch five times. When Hallie, gripped by frigid despair, drove, the ditches just drew her in. The second winter it got
better. Hallie's car stuck to the roads and she stuck to her baking.
Together the two saved her.

When you grow up in San Francisco and nearby Orinda and other
dewy places, real winter is a rude awakening. Nothing in California,
and nothing even in Prescott, Arizona, where Hallie retreated for a
while from the zany Bay Area food world, prepares you for the
withering slams of Minnesota winter. But when even a new husband
and a log cabin in Prescott aren't enough to sustain life any longer,
you move on. In the fall of 1987 Hallie left the piney quiet of
Prescott so her husband Brian could do the "fast-paced stuff" he
had been doing in nearby Phoenix—restaurant consulting and
teaching—in Crookston, where Brian had been offered a job. Not
that Crookston is so speedy, but it certainly is compared to Huot,
about fifteen miles away from Crookston with a population of six
and where the Harrons actually settled. When the Harrons arrived
in Huot the population went to eight, Brian went to work teaching
in the food-service program at the University of Crookston, and
Hallie, embarking on her first sustained taste of winter, nearly went
to pieces. By May of 1988, though, it looked like life would be

livable again. The snow stopped, the winds stopped, and one evening Hallie and Brian went to the one movie theater in Crookston. When they came out Hallie took one look and started sobbing. It was snowing.

Spring did finally follow the winter of 1988 in Huot, Minnesota, and Hallie lost no time in implementing her charted course for survival. This meant taking the one-hundred-year-old yellow shingle farmhouse she and Brian had bought and named Harronerb Farm, and opening it up to guests for lunch, dinner and lodging. When Hallie had flown from Arizona to Crookston to shop for a farm, the Harronerb idea was in her head. What better to do in the wilds of northern Minnesota than what she did best: Feed people good food. While roaming the roads outside of Crookston, Hallie had spied the Huot house with its barn and beautiful lawns and she said: "We'll take it." And they did. The thing was, there weren't a whole lot of people in Huot to invite over for dinner. And Crookston was not exactly Hitsville U.S.A., either. So Harronerb Farm would have to offer lodging in addition to good grub for the big-city folk from Minneapolis and Chicago. No sweat. Chez Panisse- and Berkeley- and San Francisco–groomed, Provence- and Tuscany-fed, all five feet of Hallie were raring to go on the sweetest (in the summer) four acres of herb, vegetable, and flower gardens north of Des Moines.

Hallie plunged in, and Huot was never the same. Out of the unsuspecting Minnesota earth appeared weird radicchios and Italian greens from seeds hauled back from Sicily that had never found a home in the Arizona sand. Nasturtiums trickled over stone walls, then went into salads, lavender nodded under the sun and found its way onto grilled beef. But in the glow of its first harvests a chill came to Harronerb Farm when the Fault Finders arrived. First came the fire inspector who spent forty-five minutes discussing *not* the fire extinguishers, *not* stove insulation. No, the subject was his wild blueberry bushes. Then came the health inspector on the day Hallie had 500 freshly baked breadsticks cooling all over the kitchen, cut-up chicken all over the counter, hungry dogs screaming, an ice cream maker cranking and no thermometer in the refrigerator. Hallie sensed doom for Harronerb Farm, but the health inspector, taking in the messy scene with a slow smile, pronounced it all fine except for the missing thermometer. Choking on her relief, Hallie swore to have it in place within twenty-four hours. Why rush, the man said; wait for a sale at Dayton's. Blessing the trusting heartland, Harronerb Farm sailed on to opening.

Hallie exercised caution at first and cooked dishes that would not seem too alien to the covered-dish crowd, things like osso buco, homemade noodles, green beans from the garden, a homemade wild blueberry ice cream and always a homemade bread along with bread sticks or *focaccia*. Noodles always brought 'em in the door, people would say, "Oh I haven't had noodles since my mother made them." As business increased Hallie grew bolder and before you knew it "these poor people from the Midwest were eating flowers and funny Italian greens in their salads and zucchini flowers with homemade ricotta." Farmers started showing up on Hallie's doorstep too as the smells from her kitchen floated over the fields. The O'Donnells brought her baby lambs fed with thyme flowers and so flavorful they seemed almost preseasoned. Hallie's chickens came from a lady farmer named Dufault who had allergies and couldn't eat store-bought chickens and raised her own without chemicals. The chicken lady's daughter Angie raised eggs and brought them over on her bicycle. One day someone showed up with a grouse. And Brian, in his spare time, would help out by ambling over to the Red Lake River to catch walleye, a bland little whitefish that Hallie would coat with sesame seeds and fry and serve with homemade potato chips. While most of the food had an Italian slant, all the flavors and ingredients were plucked from the nearby land.

And always there was the baking. Hallie baked 365 days a year. Breadsticks, 500, every other day. *Focaccia*, with saffron or garlic or rosemary, every day. Hallie had a beautiful stove to bake in, a vintage Vulcan range with six burners and a vast oven. The stove had been a gift from the city of Crookston, which was charmed to have Harronerb Farm putting the area on the map. The Vulcan had originally resided in a school kitchen on a pedestal for added height; when it was installed in Hallie's kitchen the pedestal was sent to the basement and Hallie and the Vulcan saw eye-to-eye.

Inevitably another winter came, and this time Hallie was prepared. The Vulcan radiated goodness through the whole house, and there were guests around, brave and amazing Minnesotans who would drive through white-out blizzards, arrive fifteen minutes late and then apologize. And it was in the second winter that the experience of eating with the seasons smote Hallie. Shocked into understanding, she perceived that little salads were not appealing in January. In January you wanted big beefy stews to thicken your blood. For the wise elfin cook from California, Minnesota winter revealed the essence of seasons. Still, when it was minus 35° F. outside, Hallie kept some lettuces and herbs going under the lights in the basement just for good measure. Wisdom was one thing, submission another.

In 1990 after three years devoted day and night to the farm, Hallie and Brian gave it up and moved to Minneapolis. Was it hard to give up? Only for five minutes. Hallie is a city girl after all, and farming, even gentrified farming, was "darn hard work." While Brian does his fast-paced stuff, Hallie has taken up the harp and continues her studies of Ayurveda, a form of Indian healing. She misses her raspberry bushes, though, and especially her Vulcan. It sure knew how to bake.

BAKING FOR HER LIFE

**Lettuces from Downstairs with Roasted
Peppers and Fried Eggplant Chips**

Lavender Beef

Sicilian Garlic Flans

Basil Focaccia

Young Barolo Ice

**Biscotti della Casa,
with Figs and Marsala**

———

Hallie's kitchen garden in Huot was intensive and somewhat sacred. She knew that from June through September crops would leap out of the warmed Minnesota earth and into her kitchen, but that by October the gardens outside her window would be gray again. In those four summer months, though, the abundance was astonishing. As Hallie recalls, ". . . at one point, the first season, we had to harvest the asparagus twice a day, about ten to fifteen pounds at a time. What we didn't pick in the morning, you might have used as a walking stick by late afternoon. The asparagus patch was located right next to the wild area I had designated for the various vegetable and garden nymphs, fairies and obviously the asparagus *devas*. The following year I changed the wild area and the asparagus crop was quite puny." Prolonging summer through autumn and winter meant drying herbs and flowers, freezing berries and, finally, flicking on the grow-lights for Hallie's basement garden. Harronerb Farm was its own marketplace: There wasn't another like it for at least a thousand miles.

Italian cooking often has the feel of farm life. It is slow and earthy, but delicate too. And it relies on the rich flavors of good ingredients allowed to taste of themselves. So the farmland of northern Minnesota was an ideal place for Hallie to plant her love of Italy and the following menu shows how that love blossomed. Nearly every dish has an element that must rest to acquire or exchange flavors: the peppers for the salad, the beef with its fragrant dry marinade, the peppermint in the ice, the figs and other dried fruits in marsala for the divine *biscotti*. This patient approach is what allows food to acquire layers of flavor.

If you can't find any of the newfangled lettuces listed for the salad, certainly tender hearts of butter or limestone lettuce would be fine. Hallie's recipes also often assume access to a large variety of fresh herbs but certainly dry ones can be substituted in many cases although not, obviously, for garnishes. The dry, pepper-and-herb marinade for the beef tenderloin is a helpful way to spark that otherwise fairly solemn-tasting cut of beef. Grilling it rather than roasting it, when weather allows, also adds some good charred flavors. There is no sauce for the beef, just its juices and its lavender and pepper crust. The garlic custards that accompany the beef have the gentle flavor of poached garlic.

Barolo is one of the honored wine regions of Italy and produces some of its great vintage reds. But a young Barolo with backbone is refreshing when made into a full-blooded ice. Hallie softens the wine by adding some berry purée, which will give the ice a creamier texture and make it easier to churn (alcoholic ices are sometimes tricky to freeze).

LETTUCES FROM DOWNSTAIRS WITH ROASTED PEPPERS AND FRIED EGGPLANT CHIPS

Serves 6

2 large sweet red bell peppers
2 tablespoons minced fresh marjoram, or 2 teaspoons dried marjoram
2 garlic cloves, peeled and sliced in half
1¾ cups fruity virgin olive oil
2 medium Japanese eggplant, about 8 inches long
Coarse salt and coarsely ground fresh pepper to taste
2 tablespoons lemon juice
1 tablespoon red wine vinegar
⅓ cup basil leaves
6 cups mixed small greens, cleaned and dried (arugula, oak leaf lettuce, frisé, romaine, and so on)
Marjoram sprigs
Freshly grated Parmesan cheese

Preheat the broiler.

Place the peppers on a baking sheet and broil, turning them as they blacken; the peppers may also be roasted over a gas flame. When they are totally black, place in a plastic bag until cool. Peel the peppers and remove the seeds and stems. Tear the peppers into ½-inch-wide strips and layer in a small container with the marjoram and garlic. Cover with ½ cup of the olive oil, cover, and refrigerate for at least 1 day. Bring to room temperature before finishing the salad.

Trim the ends of the eggplant and cut them either in a food processor or with a sharp knife into slices no more than ⅛ inch thick. Heat ½ cup of the olive oil to 375° F. (almost smoking). Gently drop the eggplant slices into the oil and quickly brown. Drain on paper towels and salt and pepper lightly. The eggplant chips may be kept warm for a few minutes in a 300° F. oven as the salad is finished.

In a small mixing bowl whisk together the lemon juice, vinegar and a little salt and pepper. Whisk in the remaining oil and correct the seasoning with salt and pepper. If the basil leaves are large, tear them into smaller pieces.

Place the peppers in the center of a large platter or individual plates. Toss the lettuces with the basil leaves and ¾ cup of the vinaigrette and place around the peppers. Scatter the eggplant chips on top of the peppers and in between the lettuces and drizzle the remaining dressing over all. Grind a little extra pepper over the salad, garnish with the fresh marjoram sprigs and dust with the Parmesan.

LAVENDER BEEF

Serves 6 to 8

⅓ *cup whole black peppercorns*
3 *tablespoons whole white peppercorns*
⅓ *cup fennel seeds*
1½ *teaspoons dried thyme*
3 *tablespoons dried lavender flowers (available in an herb or*
  health food store)
1 *whole beef tenderloin (prime or choice), trimmed of all fat*
  and membrane, to make 3 to 3½ pounds clean meat
Freshly minced parsley (optional)

The day before roasting the beef coarsely grind the peppercorns, herbs and lavender flowers in a small spice or coffee grinder (if you use a coffee grinder your next pot of coffee will be wonderfully fragrant). Pat the beef dry with paper towels, then rub the aromatic mixture all over the meat. Place the tenderloin in a shallow roasting pan just large enough to hold it (you may tuck under the tail of the tenderloin to help it fit; it will also roast more evenly in this position), cover with plastic wrap and refrigerate at least 24 hours. Return to room temperature 2 hours before roasting.

Preheat the oven to 375° F.

Roast the meat in the roasting pan for about 25 to 30 minutes, depending on the actual size of the roast and the temperature of your oven (for very rare beef 125° to 130° F. on a meat thermometer). Turn the meat once or twice as it cooks. Place the roast on a carving board, cover with a piece of foil and allow to rest for at least 20 minutes before carving to let the juices retract into the meat. Carve the meat, salt the slices lightly and serve drizzled with any accumulated juices. Sprinkle with a little parsley, if you wish.

SICILIAN GARLIC FLANS

Serves 6

2 large heads of garlic crushed into about 20 unpeeled cloves
¾ cup homemade chicken stock
3 eggs
1 egg yolk
½ cup heavy cream
½ cup half-and-half
¼ cup freshly grated Parmesan cheese
¾ teaspoon freshly ground pepper
2 tablespoons minced fresh chives
Salt

Lightly oil 6 ⅔-cup molds (tin baba molds or Pyrex custard cups). Place the garlic in a small saucepan with the stock and simmer, covered, over low heat for about 35 minutes, or until the garlic cloves are very tender when pierced with a knife. Remove the garlic from the pan and reserve the stock (you should have about ½ cup). Purée the garlic through the fine disk of a food mill or press it through a fine sieve using a rubber spatula.

Preheat the oven to 325° F.

In a medium mixing bowl whisk together the eggs, egg yolk, cream, half-and-half and reserved chicken stock. Add the Parmesan, pepper and chives and any salt necessary to supplement the saltiness of the cheese. Divide the custard mixture among the molds, then drop 2 teaspoons of the garlic purée into the center of each mold (any leftover purée can be saved for another use, added to scrambled eggs or omelettes, for instance). Place the molds in a shallow pan just large enough to hold them and pour enough hot water into the pan to come halfway up the sides of the molds. Bring to a simmer on top of the stove, then bake for 20 to 25 minutes, or until the center of the molds tests clean with a knife. Remove from the water bath and cool 15 minutes before unmolding. (The flans may be done ahead and gently reheated on top of the stove in the water bath.)

BASIL *FOCACCIA* (Flat Italian Bread)

Serves 8

1 package active dry or fresh yeast
1 tablespoon sugar
2 cups warm water
1 tablespoon coarse salt
½ teaspoon freshly ground white pepper
¼ cup fresh basil leaves, shredded (with fingers rather than a
*   knife)*
1 tablespoon olive oil
4 to 5 cups high-gluten (bread) flour
1 cup minced red onion
Coarse cornmeal for the baking sheet

In a large mixing bowl dissolve the yeast and the sugar in ½ cup of
the warm water. Let sit 5 minutes. Add the remaining 1½ cups
warm water, salt, pepper, basil and olive oil. Begin beating in flour,
adding enough so that the dough begins to come away from the
sides of the bowl. Turn the dough out onto a floured surface and
knead for 10 to 12 minutes, or until smooth and elastic, adding flour
as necessary to keep the dough from sticking (you may complete the
recipe to this point using an electric mixer with a dough hook
attachment if you have one). Oil a large bowl. Place the dough in
the bowl, turn to coat it with oil and let rise, covered with a towel,
for about 2½ hours, or until triple in bulk. Punch down the dough
on a lightly floured surface and knead in the onion. Return the
dough to the bowl, re-cover and let rise for 1 hour, or until doubled
in bulk.

Preheat the oven to 375° F.

Lightly oil a baking sheet. Sprinkle with the cornmeal. Punch
down the dough, place it on the baking sheet and form it into an
oval about 12 inches long and 1½ inches thick. Dimple the top of
the dough with your fingertips. Let rest 15 minutes. Drizzle the
surface of the dough with a little olive oil and bake until hollow

when thumped, about 35 minutes. Cool on a rack. Serve in slices or chunks.

YOUNG BAROLO ICE

Serves 6

2½ cups young (2- to 3-years-old) Barolo wine
About ¾ cup sugar, depending on the sweetness of the berries
2 cups strawberry or blueberry purée, or strained raspberry
*   purée*
1 tablespoon peppermint leaves, minced
Sprigs of peppermint dusted with powdered sugar

In a medium nonaluminum saucepan combine the wine and sugar and bring to the simmer to dissolve the sugar. Pour into a bowl, add the berry purée and peppermint leaves and let cool. Cover and refrigerate for at least 6 hours or overnight. Strain the mixture to remove the peppermint leaves, then freeze it in an ice cream maker. Serve in large chilled red wine goblets with the sprigs of peppermint and a platter of *biscotti* (recipe follows).

BISCOTTI DELLA CASA, WITH FIGS AND MARSALA

■■■

About 48

Grated zest of 1 lemon
½ cup golden raisins
¾ cup dried currants
½ cup dried figs (stems removed), chopped
½ cup dried apricots, chopped
½ cup marsala
1 cup unsalted butter at room temperature
2 cups sugar
4 eggs
4 cups unbleached all-purpose flour
2½ tablespoons baking powder
½ teaspoon salt
1½ tablespoons anise seeds
½ cup hazelnuts, coarsely chopped
½ cup walnuts, coarsely chopped
¼ cup anise-flavored liquor, such as Pernod

In a medium bowl combine the lemon zest, dried fruits and marsala. Let sit covered, for 24 hours, at room temperature.

In a large mixing bowl cream the butter. Add the sugar and beat until fluffy and smooth. Add the eggs and blend well. Stir in the flour, baking powder and salt. Add the dried fruit mixture, anise seeds and nuts. Refrigerate the bowl of dough for at least 45 minutes.

Place a piece of plastic wrap on a work surface. Sprinkle with 1 tablespoon of the anise-flavored liquor. Place one quarter of the dough on the plastic wrap, then shape the dough into a log about 12 inches long. Wrap the plastic around the dough and refrigerate until firm, about 4 hours. Repeat with the remaining dough to form 4 logs in all. The dough at this point may be baked or frozen for at least 1 month.

Preheat the oven to 350° F.

Bake the logs on lightly oiled baking sheets, one to a sheet (the dough will spread as it bakes), for about 25 minutes, or until browned. Remove and cool. Slice each log on the diagonal into *biscotti*. Lower the temperature to 325° F. and rebake until dry, about 10 minutes more. (For a chewier texture, the *biscotti* can be dried at room temperature rather than in the oven.) The *biscotti* are good served warm or at room temperature.

18

....

THE WYOMING

Torrington, Wyoming

In the late 1940's little Jack Canfield relied heavily on The Wyoming. The only movie theater in his hometown of Torrington in the Platte River Valley, The Wyoming was the stubby eight-year-old's personal dream machine where he bicycled most Saturday afternoons to lose himself in fantasy. The first movie he ever saw was *Bambi*, which made him cry, but at least his feelings had somewhere to go—out into the magical dark hall where wonder floated in places very far from Torrington. Stepping out from the show into the callous daylight of southeast Wyoming, Jack returned his feelings to his heart and his thoughts to his head and, reluctantly swinging onto his bike, prepared to pedal on. At least he had somewhere wonderful to pedal to, Merle's Cafe, right across the street, where he knew he'd find his Gram because that's who Merle was.

Merle's Cafe was almost as keen a destination for Jack as the movie theater. With its fantastic Western food—slabs of steak, biscuits and gravy cooking all day, big pots of coffee like Aladdin's lamps whose steam sent mouth-watering genies out the door to lure the cowboys in—Jack had a second haven where the rugged and to him bleak life of the Plains stopped at the door. Perched at the counter with his fork positioned to drift through a stack of Merle's lighter-than-heaven hotcakes, lulled by the movement of warm food around him, Jack was at ease and gazed outward. In his Gram's cafe the cowboys that appeared menacing out on the streets of Torrington and the plains of eastern Wyoming were chastened and seemed to have strolled over from the silvery world of The Wyoming.

No one—least of all Jack himself—was quite sure where the little boy with the inquisitive but guarded brown eyes, the brown hair straight as an east Wyoming high road and the curious yearnings came from. While other kids were dreaming of Gene Autry or the Lone Ranger, Jack Canfield was in France with Joan of Arc and her noble warriors. In the fourth grade two blinding but universally startling facts smote Jack. He fell in love, simultaneously and without setting one foot outside of Wyoming, with France and with Hawaii, knowing instantly that the first would become his cultural home and the second his spiritual and geographic one. He was so far gone on Joan of Arc that one day he took an old bed sheet and fashioned a great white flag emblazoned with gold *fleurs-de-lys*. His parents, Jack and Verna, were stumped: What on earth did little Jack's empassioned banner have to do with castrating cattle and shooting rattlesnakes, two of the more local tests of manhood? Clearly, not much.

There was really only one person in town who understood Jack and that was Elizabeth Clemens, a tough old Plainswoman and the local English and Latin teacher. She introduced Jack to English literature—the Brontë sisters, Dickens, Shakespeare—which eventually led to French literature and to France. Mrs. Clemens was the only educated person Jack knew and *she* certainly didn't think *fleurs-de-lys* were weird. Through her books she became Jack's sole avenue to glorious deeds, to refinement and to the altered reality that the increasingly unnerved Canfield boy, surrounded by the stark Wyoming plains, the quicksands of the Platte River and the relentless roughness of life, regularly and desperately craved.

While the ideals and lore of the Old World were seducing Jack, another world was also beckoning to him. It all began on Arthur Godfrey's morning radio show. Godfrey was a Hawaii fan and often played the ukulele and had Hawaiian entertainers on his show. Jack was mesmerized by the siren call of the Islands that wafted through the gray one-story Canfield house on the weedy edge of town. As he listened, or stared at the Dole pineapple ads in magazines, he dreamed of gentle green places and breathed exquisite air. Then, sighing, he'd put down the magazine and walk out the door to stroll on the rolling sagebrush hills, listening for meadowlarks. He knew it would be a long while, ten years or so, before he would be released from his arid life in the West. In the meantime he would wait quietly and feast on dreams.

When Jack turned ten, Tinkle McCreery gave him a further insight into his predicament. Tinkle was "a society dame" and part of the Torrington bourgeoisie. Her husband owned a lumberyard and drove an Oldsmobile 98, always a reliable sign of economic standing in the town. Working-class people like big Jack Canfield, who was the sheriff, always drove a Chevrolet, and probably a not very new one; merchants, ranchers and farmers on the other hand drove Oldsmobile 98's, and if you had really good crops or sold a lot of beef, then you glided around in a Cadillac. Anyway, one day Jack was talking to Tinkle, which was Mrs. McCreery's nickname— people in those isolated Western towns always had lots of nick- names—and puzzling over his dad who wanted a tough Western kid for a son and instead had this budding scholar. And Tinkle said, "My God, child, your parents were innocent children of Plains people when they got married, how could you expect them to know anything apart from this life?" When the Canfields and other families convened at Blue Moon Lake outside of Torrington for a good old time branding and castrating cattle and frying up Rocky Mountain oysters, Jack would conjure up his conversation with Tinkle, contemplate it a while, then shrug and tuck it away for future reference.

The wisdom of that talk escaped Jack in 1953, but it returns to him now in Hawaii, where he has lived for fifteen years and heads the Foreign Language Department at the prominent Punahou School. When Jack left Wyoming in 1965 he stayed a few years in California, where he got his Ph.D. in French at Berkeley, and then a few years abroad where he reveled in Joan of Arc's France. But all the while he was journeying to the Hawaiian Islands, which are, and always were, his utter and blissful home.

Every few years Jack revisits Wyoming, and his stay is easy there.

The tension is gone from the long horizon because he now lives beyond it. At his folks' home in Torrington, Jack's dad grins as he lines up the *white wine* next to the beer for sipping with Verna's antelope salami. Who knows, apart from some contented days with family and a taste of good Plains food, maybe Jack goes home too for a little dose of stubborn. There's plenty of that around Wyoming; it's what helped Jack get to his sweet Honolulu.

THE WYOMING

Elk Chili

Coleslaw with Basil and Caraway Dressing

Gram Merle Murphy's Chocolate Pie

When Jack Canfield says that Plains cooking has a strong identity, he is probably thinking greatly of wild game. They shoot and eat lots of it in Wyoming: antelope, elk, deer and duck. The animals that are fixtures (we hope) on the landscape are also fixtures on the table.

The menu presented here is to render respect to the traditions of great Plains settlers and to record one of the dishes that evolved out of the Plains identity. Elk chili, while a curiosity to most, is put together much like other chilis. The gamy meat adds a richer flavor that is tempered by the addition of pork. This is a familiar kind of chili—no surprises except for the elk, which is a big one. Serve it with traditional Saltines. The accompanying slaw—a sure side dish with elk chili according to Jack's aunt, Donna Gulley—contains my own noncreamy, nonsweet dressing with the green flavor of fresh basil and caraway tinted by toasting. A suggestion for a more traditional dressing is also given.

Jack's Gram Merle Murphy's chocolate pie is a one-hundred-year-old recipe. I have not toyed with or embellished it at all. It stands as a testimonial to the times when ingredients were scarce and families made do and found delight in plain things. It is a light, uncluttered pie with a frank chocolate flavor, containing only a trace amount of cocoa (by current standards), water instead of milk and few eggs. If it seems humble, it is wise to remember that this is the kind of dessert of families whose togetherness, not wealth, was the binding factor.

ELK CHILI

Serves 6 to 8

1 cup dried pinto beans, washed and soaked in water
    overnight
2½ teaspoons salt
5 cups fresh or canned tomatoes, chopped
1½ tablespoons cooking oil
2 large green bell peppers, halved, cored, seeded and chopped
2⅛ cups chopped onions
2 garlic cloves, peeled and crushed
½ cup chopped parsley
1 stick butter
2½ pounds ground elk (or venison)
1 pound lean ground pork
1 to 2 tablespoons chili powder, to taste (and depending on the
    potency of the chili powder)
Freshly ground pepper to taste

Add enough additional water to the beans to cover them and simmer
with the ½ teaspoon salt for about 2 hours, adding additional water
as necessary, until the beans are tender not mushy and most of the
water is absorbed. Stir in the tomatoes. Heat the oil in a large skillet
and sauté the green peppers and onions over medium heat for 5
minutes. Add the garlic and parsley and stir into the beans. Melt
the butter in the skillet and brown the ground elk and pork over
high heat. Add it to the bean mixture along with the chili powder,
the remaining 2 teaspoons salt and some fresh pepper. Simmer for
2 hours, stirring occasionally. Correct the seasoning with salt and
pepper. Serve with Saltine crackers.

COLESLAW WITH BASIL AND CARAWAY DRESSING

Serves 6

2 cups shredded green cabbage
2 cups shredded purple cabbage
2 large carrots, peeled and grated
½ teaspoon caraway seeds
¾ cup olive oil
1 tablespoon red wine vinegar
1 tablespoon lemon juice
2 teaspoons nonsweet mustard
8 to 10 large basil leaves, rinsed
Salt and freshly ground pepper to taste

Combine the shredded cabbages and carrots in a large bowl. Place the caraway seeds in a small skillet and roast them over medium-high heat, swirling constantly, for 1 or 2 minutes (they should darken slightly in color and have a distinct roasted aroma). Place the caraway seeds in a blender jar along with the olive oil, vinegar, lemon juice, mustard, basil leaves, ½ teaspoon salt and pepper to taste. Blend the dressing until it is fairly smooth; there will still be some flecks of basil and small bits of caraway. Pour the dressing over the cabbage mixture, stir and correct the seasoning with salt and pepper. This slaw is best eaten when freshly dressed.

Note: If you prefer a more traditional, but still nonmayonnaise dressing, the Boiled Dill Dressing on page 68, minus the chicken drippings, would be good on the slaw.

GRAM MERLE MURPHY'S CHOCOLATE PIE

■■

A 9-inch pie for 6 to 8

¾ cup sugar and ¼ cup for the meringue
1½ tablespoons unsweetened cocoa powder
¼ cup flour
2 cups hot water
Piece of butter the size of a walnut (about 2 tablespoons)
2 eggs, separated
1 teaspoon vanilla extract
1 9-inch Baked Pie Shell (see page 272)
Pinch of salt

Preheat the oven to 325° F.

In a heavy-bottomed pan stir together the 1 cup sugar, the cocoa and flour. Gradually beat in the hot water, add the butter and cook over medium heat, stirring constantly, until the mixture comes to the simmer and thickens. Remove from the heat. Stir 1 tablespoon cold water into the egg yolks, stir in a little of the hot chocolate mixture, then pour the yolks into the pan and cook and stir the custard over medium heat for another minute or two until it simmers. Remove from the heat and stir in the vanilla. Set aside to cool for ½ hour, stirring occasionally to prevent a skin from forming on the surface. Pour the custard into the baked pie shell. Beat the egg whites with the salt until they form soft peaks, then gradually add the remaining ¼ cup sugar, beating until the whites are stiff. Spread the meringue over the pie. Bake for about 15 minutes, or until nicely browned. Chill 3 or 4 hours or until set. Slice with a knife dipped in hot water.

Note: This recipe makes a thin meringue. If you prefer a more generous topping, use 4 egg whites and ½ cup sugar to make the meringue.

19

....

UNSTOPPABLE

Neahkahnie, Oregon

Near the end of June in 1984, on a tranquil hillside near the town of Plascassier in the south of France, white streamers fluttered from the olive trees. Guests from New York, Tulsa and Cannes munched on leek *tartelettes* and sipped golden Bollinger Champagne. Finally the birthday girl appeared at the door of her three hundred-year-old Provençal farmhouse, smiled, and on the arm of her husband Jean moved into the clear warmth of the Mediterranean afternoon. It was Simca—Simone Beck, the legendary cookbook author—turned eighty. Soon there was lunch, a cold tomato bisque with a caviar croûton, a garlicky lamb stew, tiny round zucchini filled with creamed sorrel, and a pretty grand raspberry and vanilla *vacherin*, all served on the stone terrace above rows of vineyards and roses. With the birthday cake the four-piece orchestra played "La Vie en Rose" then, to brighten things up, struck up "In the Mood." There was some fancy jitter-bugging under the plane trees and one couple stopped the show when she, a broad-shouldered Oregon brunette, grabbed him, an irrepressible redhead from Oklahoma, and swept him off his feet and into a torrid lunge. The audience screamed while the other couples swung back into rhythm. Simca's eightieth was a day to dance.

No one at that birthday has forgotten Emily Crumpacker's flex of her biceps when she bullied Billy Cross, a pretty bully type himself, into taking that plunge. Actually, he had no choice. As Billy found out on the dance floor: When Emily moves, you move with her. But that is not surprising in a fourth-generation Northwest woman. And if Em, as friends call her, made her mark in French food-dom and ended up close to Queen Simca, it's because back home along with strength she learned constancy, the thing that makes strength true.

It was even-keeled Ann Winkler that did it. In the late 1940's she married Peter Crumpacker and had four kids; the third, born in 1952, she named Emily. Everything went along fine until Emily turned thirteen and her dad died of pneumonia. In the years following sturdy Ann steadily sustained herself and her kids, backed up by her own resilient mother Mary Josephine Wall, known to her grandchildren as Gagi. The Crumpacker house on Riverdale Road, too, in its way added to the durability of the family. Surrounded by Douglas firs, three stories tall, it was a great engulfing beige shingle house that took everyone into its embrace.

Em and her brothers and sister loved snooping around the toolshed forts and bamboo islands of the yard and also around the neighboring house of Leata Gordon, a kind of scary lady in her eighties. Mrs. Gordon was a health food fanatic, somewhat of an oddity in the early 1960's, who to the utter incredulity of the neighborhood kids put a "treats" basket with whole raw carrots in it on her vine-covered front porch at Halloween. Even weirder, when you went to visit Mrs. Gordon she gave you celery juice to drink. Old lady Gordon was also obsessively devoted to her garden, and when she got older she would practically crawl out of her cottage in her straw hat and jeans to weed around her hydrangeas. Portland women were unstoppable.

Life for the Crumpackers, when not on Riverdale Road, was at the beach. The day that school let out in June, Ann and her bunch, along with Angus the all-purpose dog, were on the road to Neahkahnie, where Gagi had a beach house. Around the weathered gray house the summers of Em's childhood were damp, then warm, then damp again, depending on the shifts of Oregon fog. Honeysuckle vines around the house loved those shifts, and so did the blackberries, the huckleberries, the gooseberries and thimbleberries. In the sun the berries grew sweet, and in the fog their flavors grew deep; it's no wonder Oregon is famous for berries. Most mornings Em and Gagi grabbed coffee cans and went out to pick berries so Gagi could cook up a new batch of Oregon beauties for the jams she always served at breakfast with her waffles. Gagi was a resourceful cook and her beach breakfasts were famous (at least they were to her grandchildren). When she wasn't serving huckleberry waffles at the table by the big front window she was back in the kitchen baking her heavenly cinnamon rolls, simmering a fragrant stew or, when disaster struck, giving a crash course in remedial dessert work. According to Em, the first cake she ever baked had "not one air hole in it," but Gagi unswervingly resurrected it into a bread pudding. Em grew up around ingenuity. She watched her grandmother in her denim cowgirl skirt, white hair pulled into a French knot, working in a tiny beach house kitchen on a wall-mounted work table with one hinged leg, put tasty meals on the table three times a day for a ravenous mob. And back in Portland she watched her mother hold down a high school teaching job and raise four kids without breaking her stride. Even with no husband or father around, the Crumpackers not only managed, they managed well. They had a good life. They were close and contented; they were safe.

The Crumpackers stayed close to home until everyone was grown. Finally, in 1974, Em's mom for the first time ventured east of Chicago to Italy to teach on an American Army base. And Em, newly released from college with a degree in home economics and swearing never *ever* to do anything again that required a hairnet and a white uniform, went overseas herself in 1975 to visit Ann and poke around the Old World. At a cooking class in Venice she stumbled onto Julia Child who propelled Em into culinary apprenticeship in France. Em worked for two years at the Paris cooking school La Varenne, and then one day there she was, the only woman in Michel Pasquet's restaurant kitchen in the 16th *arrondissement* in Paris. Did she break her stride? Not stalwart Em, although she had a feeling she wasn't in Oregon anymore. Eventually, like most candidates in the culinary novitiate, Em met Simca, was drawn into her fold and grew close to the great lady. To Em it seemed the only natural thing: When Simca strode purposefully into the compact kitchen of her honeysuckle-covered stone farmhouse to work on her stubby table turning out beautiful food, there were glimmers of Gagi at the beach and Em was at home.

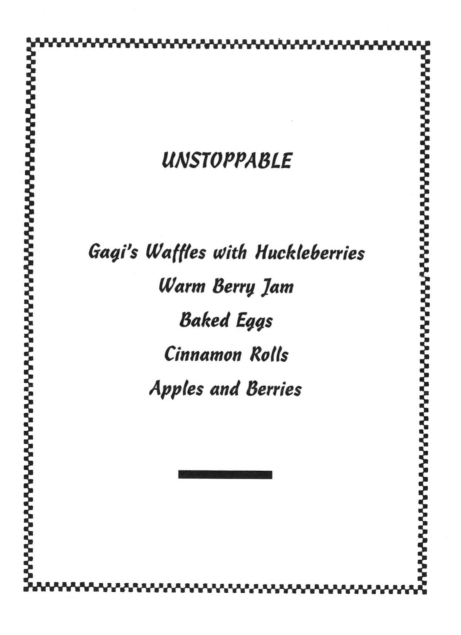

UNSTOPPABLE

Gagi's Waffles with Huckleberries

Warm Berry Jam

Baked Eggs

Cinnamon Rolls

Apples and Berries

I met Emily Crumpacker at Simca's house in Provence in December of 1980. Simca and I had arrived home weary from a 'round-the-world book-and-cook tour, but Em, as usual, was raring to go. The evening she arrived in Plascassier Em fixed me with those ebullient blue eyes, radiated a grin in my direction accompanied by the first of her many familiar ingenuous Gee Mike!'s, and before you knew it we had Simca's collection of Fred Astaire 78's stacked on the turntable and Em was guiding me through my first-ever fox trot. Oh, those starry nights of Provence when Fred and the nightingales crooned.

Em's recollection of Oregon beach breakfasts conjures up the coolness of coastal places. There are wild berries in evidence every-where—in the waffles, in the warm jams, in the platter of apples gathered behind Gagi's house. Em writes: "It was usually foggy out when we woke up at the beach, and we never knew if it would end up being a short- or long-pants day. But we did know that a hearty breakfast would be the way to begin the day. As we watched the fog roll off Neahkahnie Mountain and counted the fish printed on the seersucker tablecloth we would all wait with great anticipation for Gagi's special beach breakfast. In her waffles Gagi often used buttermilk in place of regular milk, and for an extra treat added a handful of tiny mountain huckleberries to the batter. With the waffles Gagi usually served warm jams which involved no particular method. Depending on the berries we had picked—wild huckleber-ries, blackberries, thimbleberries, or the gooseberries and blueber-ries from the patch behind the house—a jam would be created. I do remember that Gagi used two times the amount of fruit to sugar and always a squeeze of lemon. She just cooked it down, carefully stirring the mixture and lightly mashing the berries until the consis-tency she wanted was reached. It was always delicious, and at breakfast carefully distributed into each tiny waffle square. Also for special breakfasts there were Gagi's buttery baked eggs, and her cinnamon rolls, and often a plate of cold, hard, a little bit sour Mrs. Dixon apple slices garnished with the berries of the moment. Mrs. Dixon was a good friend of Gagi's who had a yard full of apple trees. She would generously invite us over to pick off the tree or the ground any apples the deer and elk had not eaten for dinner the night before."

Gagi's cinnamon rolls were made exceptional by what Em describes as "wild wonderful discoveries of clumps of cinnamon and sugar," which Gagi achieved by moistening a portion of the sugar-cinnamon mixture that was sprinkled over the dough before it was rolled. The use of a clean ironed tea towel, draped over the rolls as they rise prior to baking, is another essential grandmotherly touch. These are rather plain, homey cinnamon rolls—not wildly sticky or rich—and lovely for all those reasons. I especially recommend using the optional grated orange peel; its delicate fragrance goes very well with cinnamon.

GAGI'S WAFFLES WITH HUCKLEBERRIES

Makes 6 waffles

1¾ *cups flour*
2 *teaspoons baking powder*
½ *teaspoon salt*
2 *tablespoons sugar*
3 *eggs, separated*
1¾ *cups milk or buttermilk*
6 *tablespoons butter, melted*
½ *to 1 cup wild huckleberries*

Sift the dry ingredients into a mixing bowl. Stir together the egg yolks, milk and melted butter and add to the dry ingredients, mixing until they are just moistened. Beat the whites with a pinch of salt until they form stiff peaks, then fold them into the batter along with the berries. Cook the waffles in a preheated waffle iron lightly brushed with oil or melted butter until they are a crisp brown. Serve with soft butter and warm berry jam.

WARM BERRY JAM

∎∎∎

Makes about 3 cups

4 cups berries—wild huckleberries, blackberries,
    thimbleberries, gooseberries or blueberries
2 cups sugar (slightly more or less, according to taste)
Squeeze of lemon juice

Pick through the berries; rinse them briefly only if absolutely necessary (washing fragile berries, such as blackberries, will remove some of their juices and flavor). Place the berries, sugar and lemon juice in a large nonaluminum pot and cook over medium-low heat, stirring occasionally and lightly mashing the berries, until the sugar has dissolved and the juices are reduced and thickened slightly. The amount of time will vary, depending on the type and juiciness of the berries and the desired consistency. Runny (less cooked) jams generally have truer berry flavor and color. For the above quantities, 6 to 10 minutes of simmering should be about right but, according to your taste, the total time is variable. Serve the jam warm with the waffles. To rewarm, stir briefly over low heat in a nonaluminum saucepan. If you wish, the cooled jam can be kept in a covered container in the refrigerator for a week or so, or frozen in an airtight container.

BAKED EGGS

....

Serves 6

3 tablespoons butter, melted
6 eggs
Salt and freshly ground pepper to taste

Preheat the oven to 350° F.

Fill a flameproof baking pan with ¼ to ½ inch hot water. Place it over low heat and bring the water barely to the simmer. Divide the butter among 6 ½-cup Pyrex custard cups, crack an egg into each and season lightly with salt and pepper. Arrange the cups in the baking dish and bake until the eggs reach the desired doneness, about 6 to 8 minutes for soft eggs; 8 to 10 minutes for firmer eggs. Remove the custard cups from the baking pan, place on a small plate and serve.

CINNAMON ROLLS

....

Makes about 1 dozen

1 cup milk, scalded
2 tablespoons butter
1 tablespoon sugar
1 teaspoon salt
1 cake fresh yeast, or 1 package active dry yeast, dissolved in
    ¼ cup warm water
3 to 3½ cups unbleached all-purpose flour
Powdered sugar in a shaker (optional)

For the filling

2 tablespoons and ½ cup sugar
2½ teaspoons cinnamon
1 tablespoon chopped orange peel (optional)

Combine the hot milk, butter, sugar and salt in a large mixing bowl. When the milk mixture is just tepid, about 100° to 105° F., stir in the dissolved yeast, then beat in 1½ cups of the flour. Cover and let rise in a warm place until doubled in bulk, for about 1 hour. Stir down the batter; beat in another 1½ cups of the flour, then turn the dough out onto a lightly floured work surface. Knead for 5 or 6 minutes, adding up to ½ cup additional flour, until the dough is smooth and fairly elastic. Return the dough to the bowl and let rise again until doubled, for about 1 hour.

Punch down the dough and knead it briefly. On a lightly floured surface roll the dough out into a rectangle about 18 inches long, 11 inches wide and ¼ inch thick (the dough will be very elastic at first but will gradually relax and expand as you roll).

Prepare the filling: Stir together 2 tablespoons of the sugar and ½ teaspoon of the cinnamon and sprinkle over the dough, leaving a ½-inch border all around. Combine the remaining ½ cup sugar and 2 teaspoons cinnamon and enough drops of water to make a rough, crumbly mixture. Distribute half of this over the dough in clumps along with half of the orange peel. Dip your fingers in water and moisten the edges of the dough. Roll the dough up lengthwise and pinch the far edge to seal the dough. Cut into 12 1½-inch slices and arrange them in 2 buttered 9-inch cake pans. Cover with a clean ironed tea towel and let rise in a warm place until doubled in size.

Preheat the oven to 400° F.

Sprinkle the rolls with the remaining moist cinnamon-and-sugar mixture and the rest of the orange peel. Bake for 18 to 20 minutes. Cool on a rack for a few minutes, then invert the rolls onto a large plate. Serve warm, dusted with a little powdered sugar, and with soft butter on the side, if you wish.

APPLES AND BERRIES

■■■

Serves 6

6 to 8 crisp tart apples, peeled, cored and sliced
2 cups wild berries, such as blackberries or raspberries

Arrange the apples on a platter and garnish with the berries. Serve
cool or at room temperature.

20

....

PRAYING TO THE
SALMON SPIRIT

Olympia, Washington

OLYMPIA, WASHINGTON
January 7, 1991

Dear Mike,

Hi! Or as the dyslexic rabbi said, Yo! I was elated to hear from you.

As I write this, our latest batch of snow is melting. The yard looks like it's covered with Cool-Whip. The duck pond has stayed frozen for weeks. The ducks and geese have moved to the Sound, where the water is still liquid. At night I can hear them honking.

What's new with you and your pupperazi? Speaking of the dogs, I defrosted the fridge and found dog bones in the glacial ice. They date back from my Centralia days, do you think they improve with age? I hope they're still *al dente*. There's a photo of Blanca and Babbu on my wall. They remain high on my Most Favored Dog Status. I wouldn't mind having a mutt myself, but they're verboten here. Maybe I'll get a miniature dachshund, dress it in camo sweaters, and tell the landtrons it's a rat on steroids.

You just missed a major Northwest event: the Northwest Salmon Summit. Do you think the salmon sit at a round table or a square one?

Speaking of salmon, here's my Original Account of last December
. . . The Salmon Ceremony of the Squaxin Indians is held each year,
early in December when the last of the season's fish have been
caught. When I went, it was held in the Squaxin Tribal Center on
the reservation in Kamilche, north of Olympia. The only hint of
the impending feast was the mouth-watering smell of salmon cooking over alderwood fires. Huge chunks of fish hung suspended over
the coals.

Entering the Tribal Center, I was greeted by a woman who looked
about ninety years old. Although I'd never been there in my life
and am obviously not Native American, I felt completely welcome.
I walked back to the kitchen, offered to help and was instantly
caught up in a flurry of activity. We "waitpersons" set the long
tables with salt, pepper, paper plates and cups, nondairy creamer:
nothing out of the ordinary. But then came the food! Platter after
platter we carried it 'til there was no more room to squeeze it on
the tables. Parker House rolls and angel food cake went side by side
with bear stew and roast elk.

Meanwhile the Tribal Center was filling up with people of all
ages and tribes. I saw a Makah Indian junior high school principal;
a woman who works at the reservation's fish hatchery; a professor of
Native American Studies and his students. The warmth and hospitality seemed to fill the room to the rafters.

The first people to be seated were elders from the Makah tribe,
wearing red capes with abalone buttons. A woman in the kitchen
handed me a hot platter of salmon and asked me to set it on the
table where the Makah elders were sitting. It was so hot I could
barely keep from dropping it. Suddenly I noticed that every eye in
the room was riveted upon me—or on my platter. An elder man
began a prayer to the Salmon Spirit. I believe it was a prayer of
thanksgiving, thanking the salmon that it consented to be caught
and thus bring sustenance to the tribe as it had for centuries. But
it was hard for me to maintain reverent attention when I was holding
a burning hot platter, not knowing if I could put it down without
offending my hosts, let alone the Salmon Spirit.

Finally the prayer ended and we all sat down to eat. The conversation was as wonderful as the food. When everyone had finished

eating they cleared the tables as if by unspoken command. Within minutes, it seemed, the food-laden tables were replaced by rows of chairs.

The Makah elders began to dance, accompanying themselves with drums on which animals were painted. The elders must have been at least seventy years old, but their faces glowed and they danced with ease. It was apparent that this culture respects and cherishes its old people. Next was a potlatch. This was traditionally a way that wealthier Indians redistributed wealth by giving away their surplus. At this potlatch, I didn't know the source or meaning of the things that were given away. All I know is that young women walked from person to person, giving away fishnets, glassware, handkerchiefs and oranges. At the end of the potlatch we were invited to come to the kitchen and take home any leftovers we wanted. I took a huge piece of roasted salmon.

Well, now you've got the scoop. Incidentally, the Squaxins also have a Welcoming Ceremony for the salmon in July, at a local dock. I saw it advertised in the paper—it's free, everyone welcome—I hope to go this year. Care to join me?

If things go as planned, I'm hoping to take the Alaska Marine Highway to Juneau and back in mid-June. The ferries let people sleep on deck. From what I've heard, nobody wants to sleep anyway since it's daylight all night.

In the meantime I might start working at Potlatch State Park. It's in the Skokomish Indian Reservation on a fjord. The job would include maintaining the grounds, collecting fees and enforcing the law. Somehow when I minored in Native American Studies, I didn't expect to be issuing citations for crimes like "unauthorized disposal of fish parts." Frankly I'd prefer to take bribes from any poachers, in the form of the oysters, clams and crabs they catch on the sly.

That's all for now. I hope you stay in touch. Regards to all (two-footed and four-footed).

Love,

Beck

PRAYING TO THE SALMON SPIRIT

Bear Stew for 4,000
Bear Stew for 6 to 8

Beck and I grew up together in Berkeley. The moment she walked into my kindergarten class at Oxford Elementary School I knew I had a pal for life. Beck had a grin gleaming with mischief, a heart loaded with loyalty, and when she tossed her brown pigtails back over her shoulders and, sucking in air, belched like a queen, I knew I had found royalty in the rough. North Berkeley was an incredible woodsy kingdom for Beck and me. Through the oak and eucalyptus groves of Live Oak Park, the heady drops of Terrace Walk, and the tangled yards of Mariposa and Shattuck streets, we scampered tirelessly in the footsteps of our hero Nancy Drew, searching for clues in crumbling walls, conjuring up sinister signposts. I guess we didn't want to grow up very much; it was sobering when Beck's pigtails gave way to a bob, and our clubhouse, The Gig Cottage (named after my *nom de sleuth*), was padlocked for the last time. But we still sometimes meet for adventures up on the Yuba River, Beck and I, and she always keeps me posted on local life in Washington, where she now lives. Beck's evening at the Salmon Ceremony was one of her recent bold undertakings.

I decided on a recipe for bear stew for this chapter because, while it may seem a curiosity (or an atrocity) to many, to Northwest Native Americans as well as certain newcomers among them, bear stew is part of a tradition of life in the wilderness. Whether or not you ever make a bear stew is not really important, since the procedure is essentially the same as for a good beef stew, always a worthwhile dish to have under your belt. In fact, bear stew is often made with only some bear meat and the rest beef chuck, especially if you are making it for a large group, as Ron Pittman of McCleary, Washington, has for almost fifteen years.

I tracked down Ron Pittman after inquiring at the Squaxin Tribal Center for a bear stew expert. Ron is definitely that, and conveyed in a few words his years of bear stew-making for the annual Bear Festival in McCleary. Like the Salmon Ceremony, the Bear Festival celebrates not the killing of wild animals but rather their place in nature and in the cycles of Native American life. The harmony, not supremacy, of humans with animals is implied. When Ron Pittman makes stew for 4,000 for the Bear Festival, it takes a few days, and he has plenty of assistants, and the cooking goes on 'round the clock. By six o'clock in the evening on the third Saturday in July, 550 gallons of rich brown bear stew are ready for the tables, and Ron, who has worked all night and all day, pulls up a chair. I have included verbatim the Bear Festival recipe for bear stew, since it kind of takes your breath away, and then followed it with a vastly reduced version that calls for pots and pans, not vats. The "spice pot" in the Festival recipe, by the way, is deliberately vague, and is something concocted every year by the local high school kitchen. Ron wasn't saying too much about it, implying, I guess, an invitation to come to McCleary and sample the real stuff. Since James Beard calls bear "one of the most delicious of game animals," maybe we'll see you there.

BEAR STEW FOR 4,000

••

For about 550 gallons

200 pounds bear meat
400 pounds beef chuck
200 pounds carrots, peeled
1 crate celery
225 pounds yellow onions, peeled
550 pounds boiling potatoes, peeled and cut in quarters
2 crates cabbage, sliced into wedges
Salt and freshly ground pepper to taste
20 gallons "spice pot"—parsley, oregano, cloves, garlic—you
  name it

As friends bring you bear meat, freeze or can it. A couple of days before your guests arrive, assemble 10 assistants, brown the bear meat and beef chuck in oil, then the carrots, celery and onions, cut up. Stew the meat in several large vats covered with water for about 3 hours, until the meat is tender. Add the aromatic vegetables along with the potatoes and cabbage, season lightly, and simmer for another hour or so, until the meat and vegetables are very tender. Skim off the fat, make the gravy, and flavor to taste with "spice pot." Set the table for 4,000 and serve.

BEAR STEW FOR 6 TO 8

Makes about 1 gallon

1½ pounds bear meat, all fat removed and cut into 4-ounce
    pieces
3 pounds beef chuck, all fat removed and cut into 4-ounce
    pieces
About ¾ cup olive oil
Salt and freshly ground pepper to taste
2 carrots, scrubbed and chopped
3 stalks celery, washed and chopped
1 pound yellow onions, peeled and sliced
5 tablespoons flour
½ cup bourbon
1 bottle good red wine (a hearty Zinfandel)
2 quarts homemade beef stock or water
Several sprigs of parsley
Several branches of fresh thyme, or 1 teaspoon dried thyme
6 juniper berries
2 bay leaves
6 garlic cloves, crushed
3 or 4 whole cloves
2 pounds red or white boiling potatoes, washed and quartered
1 small green cabbage, cut into wedges
1 pound small carrots, peeled and rinsed
1 pint pearl onions, dropped in boiling water for 30 seconds,
    drained and peeled
1 tablespoon cracked fresh pepper
1 tablespoon fresh thyme or rosemary leaves, chopped,
    or 1 teaspoon dried

Preheat the oven to 325° F.

Pat the meat dry with paper towels. Heat 4 tablespoons of the
olive oil in a large 8- to 10-quart heavy-bottomed pot set over high

heat and brown the meat on all sides in several batches, taking care not to crowd the pan (or else the meat will steam rather than sear). Add additional oil to the pan as necessary. As the pieces of meat are browned, set them aside and season lightly. Add more oil to the pan, stir in the carrots, celery and onions and stir them over medium-high heat until they are lightly browned. Remove the vegetables from the pan. Add 4 tablespoons of olive oil, then stir in the flour and cook over medium-low heat, stirring constantly, until the *roux* is medium brown. Return the meat and vegetables to the pan, add the bourbon, then the bottle of wine and simmer for 1 or 2 minutes. Pour in enough stock or water to cover. Add the parsley, thyme, juniper berries, bay leaves, garlic and whole cloves. Bring to the simmer, place a piece of parchment paper or wax paper over the meat, cover with the lid and bake for about 2 hours (regulate the heat so the liquid remains at a steady simmer). When the meat is very tender, remove it to a bowl and cover with the piece of parchment paper (if any cloves remain with the meat, discard them). Strain the liquid through a fine sieve, pressing down on the aromatic ingredients with a spoon to extract all of their flavor. Thoroughly degrease the liquid and return it to the pan. Boil it down rapidly until you have about 4 cups, skimming the gravy occasionally as it reduces.

While the gravy is simmering, steam the potatoes and then the cabbage until tender; season lightly with salt and pepper. In a large skillet heat 2 tablespoons olive oil. Add the carrots and pearl onions, season lightly and toss or stir them together to coat with the oil. Add 3 or 4 tablespoons simmering bear gravy to the pan, cover, and stew gently for 25 to 30 minutes, or until the carrots and onions are tender.

When the gravy is the right consistency, season it, return the meat to the pot, add the onions and carrots and stir all together. Simmer for at least 10 minutes so all the flavors can blend together. Correct the seasoning with salt and pepper. Serve the stew, sprinkled with the pepper and thyme or rosemary, from the pot or on a hot platter. Surround with the potatoes and cabbage that have been basted with a little of the hot gravy. The stew will actually be better served a day or two after it is made.

21
....

HIGH OCTANE

La Crescenta, California

I f along about 1941 you had been cruising down Foothill Boulevard in Flintridge, California, and found yourself running low on gas, chances are you would have spotted Peverill's Union Oil Station and pulled up to the pumps. In those rationed wartime years, four gallons of gas per person per week was it, and the quip "fill 'er up" was rapidly becoming quaint from disuse. But if a lanky young blond woman attendant about twenty years old with eyes blue as a southern wave had strode over to the pump and cranked it up for action, you might have slipped from behind the wheel and sauntered around the rear bumper for a chat, hoping to charm Marion Enwright out of an extra gallon or two. You would have been wrong.

"Everybody tried to kid me out of that gasoline, everybody wanted more," Marion now chuckles. "I heard every story in the book, they tried everything. They didn't try ice cream, though. They should have."

Running that southern California service station was serious business for the woman who, thirty-five years later, would become a prominent exponent of American cooking and a best-selling writer of cookbooks. Getting that job, her first steady one after finishing high school, just about saved her life. A disastrous freshman year at Glendale College convinced Marion to forget about school. She was too restless to sit in a classroom any longer. So there Marion was, at the age of nineteen about as desperate as she could get. All her friends could keep jobs and she couldn't. No job could harness her colossal horsepower.

Then one day Marion was rifling through the pages of the *La Crescenta Ledger* (her hometown paper) and saw this big ad that said, "Replace a man for the War. Union 76 wants you." All the young gas station attendants had gone off to fight, and the oil company was recruiting women to pump gas for their country. A light went on in Marion's head. She sped off to Flintridge and since no one else answered the ad (there weren't many women around who were keen on pumping gas) she landed the job and loved it from the first minute. Working an eighteen-hour day, Marion went home, for the first time in her life, happily worn out. She was a blur around that gas station, changing tires, changing *truck* tires, cleaning spark plugs, doing a t-and-d (transmission and differential oil change) and, of course, pumping gas. And the sight of her—a purposeful five foot ten, smooth blond hair pulled right back, smile as sunny as a Laguna day—must have stopped hardened grease monkeys, along with the customers, dead in their tracks. After about six months on the job Marion took over the running of the station when Peverill, the station owner, became bed-ridden with a back injury. That Union Oil Station really began to boogy with its new top gun at the controls. Before long, Dottie Flanagan, one of Marion's pals, hired on. The truckers stared and growled in disbelief. Two women running the show? But when they got good service *and* a radiant grin, the truckers grinned back.

"I just loved cars. I still like cars," confirms Marion. "Ever since then I always thought I'd buy a service station. You can talk all day to people in one. See, that's the other thing I loved about that gas station back in Flintridge. I liked meeting all the people who came and went."

Marion's curiosity about people began while she was growing up in the foothill town of La Crescenta, which for years was a haven for "lung'rs," people with weak chests or bad lungs. Marion, a robust and energetic child, wasn't a "lung'r," but her Italian mother Mary Spelta Enwright was, as a result of an early bout of tuberculosis. In 1934 she moved her husband and her only child from Los

Angeles to the healthy climate of La Crescenta near the San Gabriel Mountains twenty-five miles northeast of the city. Twelve-year-old Marion loved the early-California feel of La Crescenta, with its perfumed orange trees, its pepper and olive trees. Her Irish father, Joseph Enwright, suffered from Buerger's disease, a rare and severe disorder of the arteries, which made him an invalid at the age of thirty. Although he had never in his life tinkered with anything more taxing than a crystal radio set, Joseph rose to the occasion and designed a compact one-and-one-half-story Spanish-style house. It had a small living room, tiny dining room and kitchen, and at the top of five steps there were two bedrooms. Those steps now appear as a refuge in Marion's memory. When the warm Santa Ana winds rushed around the house on nights during the Great Depression, Marion, on some 3 A.M. expedition, often found her father huddled and trembling on the fifth step, a frail man made uneasy by the sound of wind.

Apart from the house designed by her father, what Marion loved most about the town was that it was filled with all kinds of people: families, loners, local heros and lunatics. La Crescenta had it all. Just a few blocks away there was the Rice family, with fifteen children and no money. Then near the Rices' was the Bissell vacuum cleaner family living in a mansion. And there was Mr. Gillespie who dug cesspools even though he had a weak chest. One neighbor, Robert Reed, used to build his own dynamite, then once a year buy an old wreck of a car and blow it up at midnight. No one cared. La Crescenta in the 1930's was a very tolerant place, and no respecter of economics—rich or poor. If people had bad lungs, La Crescenta was where they went. When people behaved a little crazy, no one minded, as long as no one got hurt.

If Marion liked the oddballs of La Crescenta, that suited them fine, because they really doted on her too. Most of the town's inhabitants, being "lung'rs," were older and often a little lonely. Fearless Marion, of the gleaming aqua eyes and blazing warm laugh, did a dandy job of cheering folks up. Many afternoons she'd spend playing ball with Mrs. Monahan's two old sons who had lung damage from working in the mines back East somewhere. From ball practice Marion would often trot for a snack over to the little service station with two pumps where Grace something-or-other lived. Her house was attached to the service station, and she taught Marion how to play cribbage. Along with the cribbage came fancy little bridge sandwiches cut in the shape of a heart or a diamond, a club or a spade, and they'd be filled with tuna, or sometimes peanut butter, all of which Marion loved. Marion liked food, and was thinking about it a lot.

Marion began thinking about food when she began *reading* about food. "I loved *Little Women*, because Meg and Jo were always making all that *blancmange* to take to Laurie who was ill. Then there was Heidi, who would sit on a stool in her grandfather's house in Switzerland and eat goat cheese." Books opened up the world of food for Marion in a way her homelife didn't. Surprisingly for an Italian, Marion's mother was not much of a cook. Joseph Enwright was not much of an eater, he was a drinker, and as a result the Enwright household stuck pretty much to meat and potatoes. Once in a while Mary Enwright rebelled and served a big platter of spaghetti. Marion remembers her mother's tomato sauce in thin pots, bubbling forever. Other than spaghetti, Marion didn't taste much Italian food as a child unless it was her grandmother's artichokes stuffed with fried breadcrumbs or her delicate ribbon cookies, served on special occasions.

Marion left La Crescenta in 1942 when she married her childhood friend Robert Cunningham, a compact, good-hearted man with western-sky blue eyes and a mischievous grin. The newlyweds set up housekeeping down in San Diego so Robert could report for duty at El Toro Naval Station. Marion, fresh from her conquests at Peverill's gas station in Flintridge, hired right on with Union Oil in San Diego. She still loved being in a service station; Robert thought it was a mess. He would wash all of her uniforms and they *were* a mess. And no matter how she scrubbed herself Marion always smelled like 40-weight oil. It was in her pores, in her hair, and no shampoo in the world could get that smell out. When Marion wasn't busy being Mrs. Goodwrench, at home she was confronting the challenges of running a house, which included, naturally, learning how to cook. With her customary resolute good sense Marion quickly devised a system. "I learned to cook by asking neighbors what *they* cooked," Marion recalls. "I really liked getting recipes from people, it was a nice way to get introduced. I remember one woman who told me exactly how to stuff a pork chop and fry it. It was one of my very first successes, very simple but good. It had marjoram in it, and onion, and then a milk gravy was made with the drippings. Pretty soon I had a notebook with all these neighbors' recipes." Just as it did in her childhood, Marion's curiosity about people enriched her life.

While Marion was picking the brains of all the neighborhood cooks, Robert was often her reluctant guinea pig. He wasn't too interested in eating. His favorite menu was burnt steak and bourbon. He didn't want to see anything green around, he used to say, unless it was money. He liked meat and he liked sweets, period. He especially liked custard pies, like lemon or banana cream. Back then, Marion didn't know how tricky those pies were so she never worried about it. She just made them. "If the pies weren't good, we didn't know it. We didn't think like that then. We didn't dissect things then, nobody's palate was jaded, nor was anyone a food critic. I always felt, you can eat it even if it doesn't work out, it's always worth tasting."

When the war came to an end in 1945 Marion left gas station work for good. She and Robert moved north and raised some kids, and while Robert was busy becoming a big-shot lawyer, Marion began to write cookbooks and become famous. California in the seventies and eighties was bursting with flavor and Marion had her own ingredients to add to the stew. But it was the talk and companionship around food, not the fame, that always warmed her life. The bold, little blond girl of La Crescenta in the thirties, munching bridge sandwiches and streamlining her game of cribbage, had sensed that then and always would.

HIGH OCTANE

Stuffed Pork Chops with Pineapple-Orange Dressing and Pan Gravy

Buttermilk Biscuits

Buttered Green Beans with Sage and Thyme

Maple Yams

Banana Custard Pie

Marion's stuffed pork chops are the homey kind that bake until the meat is falling off the bone. Double-thick shoulder chops are delicious for this kind of long slow cooking as the meat, being on the gelatinous side, remains moist. Loins chops will do nicely also. The bread dressing is slightly sweet with fresh pineapple, which if you can find it very ripe, is worth using for its delicate perfume. If any of the dressing squeezes out of the chops into the pan while they bake, it will be a good addition to the gravy made at the end. The gravy, by the way, can be made less rich by using a homemade broth in place of the milk. The biscuits, made with buttermilk, are fluffy and have a pleasing, faintly sour taste.

Green beans are a good accompaniment to pork. In this simple version they are buttered and given some interest by the addition of two of what I like to call the "dusty" (earthy) herbs, sage and thyme. I have added some of my own maple yams to this menu. They are only a little sweet, and keep their texture by being sliced rather than mashed or puréed.

A homemade banana custard pie can be delectable in a way that a store- or bakery-bought pie cannot. What makes a pie perishable, its tenderness, is also what makes it fine. The egg yolk custard in this pie has just enough flour to support the yolks and thicken the custard without weighing it down. This is what a friend calls a "right-now pie," because it is really ready only once—when it is just finished, cool and not cold, with its soft flavors settling over the dry crust.

STUFFED PORK CHOPS WITH PINEAPPLE-ORANGE DRESSING AND PAN GRAVY

▪▪

Serves 6

2 tablespoons cooking oil
6 shoulder or loin pork chops about 2 inches thick, trimmed of
*   fat, slit in the middle for pockets*
Salt and freshly ground pepper to taste
2 cups dry fresh bread crumbs
2 teaspoons chopped fresh marjoram, or 1 teaspoon dried
*   marjoram*
¼ cup chopped celery, leaves included
2 tablespoons finely minced onion
3 tablespoons butter, melted
½ cup chopped fresh pineapple
2 teaspoons grated orange rind
½ cup hot water

Heat the oil in a large ovenproof skillet. Pat the pork chops dry with paper towels, salt and pepper them, then brown them over medium-high heat on both sides. Remove the chops from the skillet and allow them to stand until cool enough to handle. Pour out the fat from the skillet.

Combine the bread crumbs, marjoram, celery, onion, melted butter, pineapple and orange rind, season with about ¾ teaspoon of salt and some pepper and toss to mix well. Fill each pork chop pocket with the stuffing; secure the pockets by inserting one or two toothpicks through each chop.

Preheat the oven to 350° F.

Place the pork chops back in the skillet in a single layer, add the hot water, cover with a lid or a piece of foil and bake for 1½ hours. Add a little more water during baking, if needed. When the chops are done, remove to a serving dish, discard the toothpicks and keep warm. Pour the liquid from the skillet into a small bowl or measuring cup and remove the fat from the surface, reserving 2 tablespoons for the pan gravy. Prepare the gravy (recipe follows) and pass it with the pork chops and the buttermilk biscuits.

PAN GRAVY

About 3 cups

2 tablespoons fat from the pork cooking liquid
2 tablespoons flour
2½ cups milk or good chicken broth
The reserved cooking liquid
2 teaspoons chopped fresh marjoram, or 1 teaspoon dried
    marjoram
Salt and freshly ground pepper to taste

Add the fat to the skillet and stir in the flour; cook over low heat, stirring steadily, for 1 or 2 minutes. Beat in the milk or broth and the pork cooking liquid, raise the heat and bring to the simmer, whisking steadily, until the gravy has thickened and is smooth. Cook for a few minutes over low heat, scraping the bottom and sides of the skillet to dissolve any baked-on juices. If any stuffing from the chops remains in the pan, it will be delicious in the gravy. Add the marjoram, correct the seasoning with salt and pepper and serve.

BUTTERMILK BISCUITS

••

Approximately 16 biscuits

2 cups unbleached all-purpose flour
½ teaspoon salt
2 teaspoons baking powder
½ teaspoon baking soda
½ cup solid vegetable shortening
⅔ cup buttermilk

Preheat the oven to 425° F.

Combine the flour, salt, baking powder and baking soda in a mixing bowl and stir them together with a fork. Drop the shortening into the dry ingredients and, using 2 knives or your fingertips, work the shortening into the dry ingredients until the mixture is in fine, irregular crumbs resembling soft bread crumbs. Add the buttermilk all at once and stir with a fork just until the dough forms a cohesive mass.

Turn the dough out onto a smooth lightly floured surface and knead 12 to 14 times (about a minute). Pat into an 8 × 8-inch square about ½ inch thick, and, using a knife, cut the dough into 2-inch squares. Place the biscuits on an ungreased baking sheet (with biscuits touching if you want them light and fluffy, or at least 1 inch apart if you want them darker and crisper). Bake for 15 to 18 minutes and serve very hot.

BUTTERED GREEN BEANS WITH SAGE AND THYME

▪▪

Serves 6

2 pounds green beans, washed, stems and strings removed
4 to 5 tablespoons butter
Salt and freshly ground pepper to taste
2 teaspoons fresh chopped sage, or ¼ teaspoon dried sage
1 teaspoon fresh thyme leaves, or ¼ teaspoon dried thyme
    leaves

Cook the green beans in a large quantity of boiling salted water until tender, about 5 to 8 minutes, depending on the type and size of bean. Drain thoroughly; if the beans are not to be eaten immediately, rinse them in cold water to stop the cooking. Just before serving, melt the butter in a large skillet, add the green beans and stir or toss them until they are hot and nicely coated with the butter. Season to taste with salt and pepper, add the herbs and serve.

MAPLE YAMS

∎∎

Serves 6

6 tablespoons butter
2 pounds yams or sweet potatoes, peeled and cut into ⅛-inch-
thick slices
1¼ teaspoons salt
Freshly ground pepper to taste
3 or 4 tablespoons maple syrup
3 or 4 tablespoons heavy cream (optional)
1 teaspoon chopped fresh thyme leaves, or ¼ teaspoon dried
thyme leaves

Melt the butter in a large preferably nonstick skillet. Add the yams or sweet potatoes and seasonings and toss or stir to coat the potatoes well with the butter. Cook for about 30 minutes over medium heat, stirring or tossing frequently; the potatoes will brown and caramelize slightly. When they are tender, add the maple syrup and continue cooking for another 5 to 10 minutes. Watch the potatoes closely at this point as the maple syrup will make them take on color much more rapidly. Add the cream, if desired, and the thyme, cook another 3 minutes, correct the seasoning with salt and pepper and serve. (The maple yams may be prepared in advance, placed in a shallow baking dish and rewarmed in a 400° F. oven for 6 to 8 minutes just before serving.)

BANANA CUSTARD PIE

■■

One 9-inch pie for 8

4 *eggs yolks*
⅔ *cup sugar*
¼ *teaspoon salt*
3 *tablespoons flour*
2 *cups hot milk*
2 *teaspoons vanilla extract*
1½ *tablespoons butter, melted*
1 *9-inch fully baked, pie shell (recipe follows), cooled*
2 *bananas, sliced*
1 *cup heavy cream, beaten to soft peaks with 2 tablespoons*
sugar and 1 teaspoon vanilla extract

In a mixing bowl beat the egg yolks until they are slightly thick, then gradually beat in the sugar. Stir in the salt and the flour. Slowly add the hot milk to the egg mixture, stirring constantly, then pour into a heavy-bottomed saucepan and cook over moderate heat, stirring constantly, until thickened. Remove from the heat and pour back into the mixing bowl. Stir in the vanilla. Pour the melted butter over the custard and spread it evenly over the surface to prevent a skin from forming. Cover the bowl and refrigerate until cool. Shortly before serving, cover the bottom of the baked pie shell with sliced bananas. Add the cool custard, smoothing it evenly with a spatula. Cover with the whipped cream and serve.

BAKED PIE SHELL

One 9-inch shell

1 cup unbleached all-purpose flour
¼ teaspoon salt
⅓ cup vegetable shortening
2 to 3 tablespoons cold water

In a mixing bowl stir together the flour and salt. Drop the shortening into the dry ingredients and, using your fingertips, work the shortening into the flour mixture until it is in coarse, irregular crumbs. Stir in just enough cold water, using a fork or your fingers, so that the mixture will form into a rough ball.

On a lightly floured surface roll out the dough into an 11- to 12-inch circle. Fit the rolled piece of dough loosely into a 9-inch glass or metal pie plate, pushing the dough down the sides of the pan rather than stretching it (if it is stretched, it will tend to shrink when it is baked). Tuck the rough edges of the dough under to form a smooth border, then press an attractive pattern around the rim of the dough. Prick the bottom and sides of the shell with a fork. Set in the freezer to firm up for 15 minutes. The shell may be covered with foil and frozen at this point, then put directly into the hot oven (in which case the baking time should be increased by 2 or 3 minutes).

Preheat the oven to 450° F.

Bake the pie shell for 5 or 6 minutes, then lower the heat to 400° F. and continue baking it for another 10 to 12 minutes, or until the shell is lightly golden. If the dough bubbles during the baking, prick the bubble with a fork and gently press out the air. Set on a rack to cool.

22

....

TURIE

Monterey, California

S tanding on Spaghetti Hill in Monterey is a good way to know about Italians. Below the hill is the curve of spacious wealthy bay that a hundred years ago attracted the Italians to fish it, and on the hill is where many of them settled, so they could eternally watch the water. If Italians, as the film writer Pauline Kael once said, have a talent for babies, they also have a talent for the sea.

Back down on the flats of town and out along Wharf #1 there works a curly-haired little man with a grand name, Bonaventura Cavaliere, who is a keeper of that talent. You can't pronounce his name in one breath, you say? Well, neither can anyone else, so just call him Turie for short. A new customer progressing along the wharf and dodging the pink wands of cotton candy carriers can easily miss the wooden Cavalier Market sign with the letters curving like a fish and the last "e" missing (the sign-maker reached the tail before he could finish the name, but the sign stayed anyway). But it wouldn't matter because he could follow the path of people, not strolling like out-of-towners, but *striding* right up to Turie's place to collect on the Cavaliere promise of good fish from Monterey. Turie knows good fish; it's his life. If his squid, or bay salmon, or Monterey prawns aren't proof enough, the large blurry black-and-white photograph that hangs in the shop, of a six-year-old Turie in front of his dad's fish counter in Watsonville back in the 1950's, should be. Wearing his boy-size apron and the slight squint of the warm lands, he is the New World telling of an old Italian story.

While the haunting Monterey scenery might have drawn many immigrant families at the start of the century, for the Italians, many of them Sicilian, scenery had nothing to do with it. Sardines were the magnet, plain and simple. What they had fished around Palermo, sardines and mackerel and squid, Turie's grandparents could fish around Monterey and that suited them fine. The Cavalieres had originally journeyed from Sicily to Pittsburgh, California, to fish salmon in the brackish waters of the delta. When the steel mills came the salmon slowed down and the Cavaliere clan looked for a happier hunting ground, which they and other *Siciliani* found in the calm coastal life of central California. In the nearly unfathomable waters of the great Monterey Bay, relocated Italian families renewed their bond with the sea. Their Italian talents had a home again: They fished, babies were born, babies grew up and were drawn to the sea.

Well, not all babies. Turie's father, born Ratzi Cavaliere in 1921, was that odd Sicilian: He retreated from the sea. Ratzi was the first of a generation that would strive for something else. He learned retailing in the mom-and-pop groceries around Monterey, and eventually opened his own fish market in Watsonville twenty miles up the coast. The only time Ratzi Cavaliere actually did go to sea was during World War II when fishermen, as essential food providers, were granted rare draft deferments. Viewing his family's trade as his contribution to his adopted nation's defense, and possibly sensing that the theater of the near Pacific was a safer proposition than the theater of the South Pacific, Ratzi willingly fished during the war years. By the time Turie was born in 1947, his father had retired from the sea and with his mother had settled into the family market in Watsonville. To Ratzi being a fish seller, not a fisherman, was progress. His small-town business prospered thanks to the large populations around Watsonville of Filipino and Japanese farm laborers and food processing plant workers who included fish in their diet almost daily. Oddly, Monterey was not a big fish-eating town; nearly all the local fish was shipped around the country, or else processed for shipment around the world. The only real fish-eaters in Monterey were, naturally enough, the Italians, and do you think they'd accept fish from a fish market? Heaven forbid. No, every family had its own boat which kept the inhabitants of Spaghetti Hill steadily fed with fresh *frutti di mare*. Up in Watsonville, however, fish retailing was a going thing, and as he was growing up Turie spent his weekends helping out Ratzi, and occasionally standing on tiptoe to dip into the till. Hanging around his dad, learning the fish trade, sharing in the wealth—all pretty normal in the life of an Italian kid.

Ratzi Cavaliere—whose nickname, ironically, was Skipper, a fabrication he loved to perpetuate as much to uphold the family's honor as fishermen as to thumb his nose at it—ultimately tried to dislodge his son from the fish business, but Turie stood firm. College was not for him. Turie's mother Sarah, "a good chunky woman," also stood firm: If her son was going to remain in the family business, he was not going to drive forty treacherous miles every day along the Coast Highway to Watsonville and back. It was bad enough that she and Ratzi had done it all those years; Turie would have it easier. In 1972 the Cavalieres sold their Watsonville market— urban renewal had come along and was reshaping the business district anyway—and shortly after resettled their business on the Monterey wharf. Monterey was no longer mainly a blue collar and military town; it was now also a place for leisure frequented by a gentrified population attuned to seafood. The fortunes of the California central coast shifted in the seventies and eighties, and the Cavalieres shifted amiably along with them.

Like the hills of North Beach in San Francisco, the hills of Monterey seem a little less Italian now. "You lose your tradition," Turie notes philosophically enough but with a tinge of sadness in his eyes. Sarah Cavaliere died in May of 1990, and the day marked a change in the life of the compact Italian man down on Wharf #1. Italian mothers are the hub of their families, and with Sarah gone the Cavaliere family has dissolved a little bit. But if Italians live well they also remember well, and Turie senses his mother every day as he strides to work along the wharf with the maternal slopes of the town behind him.

TURIE

*Ravioli with Ricotta and
Fresh Tomato Compote*

Grilled Salmon with Bread Crumbs

*Young Arugula and Other Greens,
with Lemon and Olive Oil*

Nana Sarah's Sponge Cake

———

Thursdays and Sundays were always red spaghetti days in Monterey. According to some unspoken law, Italian families on the central coast always ate spaghetti with tomato sauce on those days. So it stood to reason that you got a little tired of all that cooked tomato sauce. The warm tomato compote that accompanies the ricotta and herb ravioli in the following menu is a far cry from "red sauce." Made with chopped fresh tomatoes—even slightly out of season tomatoes—that are simply warmed in olive oil with a few herbs, this kind of compote has a clear tomato flavor—both acid and sweet—and a fresh texture that heavy tomato reductions don't have. Some Italian cooks sometimes simply warm the chopped tomatoes and olive oil in the hot sun; which is to say how fine and simple this treatment of tomatoes is. The ravioli that go under the tomatoes—and which, on Spaghetti Hill in Monterey, were made on special holidays by Italian mothers and aunts and grandmothers cooking together—are plump with ricotta, a little Parmesan and basil. Nothing else. Homemade pasta, especially hand-rolled pasta, is so wonderful it always seems best to accompany it with only a few flavors. Homemade pasta is not difficult to make: You can mix and roll it by hand, or you can use machines; either gives a good result. The egg dough used for ravioli, made with unbleached all-purpose flour, is easier to roll and slightly softer and fluffier when cooked than doughs made with high-gluten durum wheat flour (semolina). There is a lot to say about pasta-making. The instructions given here are elemental but adequate; for more details on the subject, Marcella Hazan's cookbooks are an excellent source.

The children of Italian-American fishing families don't eat much fish nowadays. Turie's kids are like other kids who would rather eat hamburgers and hot dogs, although they will eat fish when it is served, stoically and out of respect, if not out of preference. But during Turie's childhood, before the days of food crazes, a special boneless filet of halibut or snapper pan fried was something he expected and liked. One of the great delicacies of the Cavaliere kitchen was Monterey Bay salmon steaks that were moistened with olive oil, coated with homemade bread crumbs and cooked on the barbecue. This unusual and absolutely simple preparation of salmon is one of the best you will ever eat. The slight smoky flavor and the crisp crumbs make the tender fish delectable. A simple salad with lemon and olive oil is all that's needed with the fish since the ravioli course provides both starch and vegetable. It is very Italian to serve the main course basically unadorned, so you savor it more.

Desserts don't play a large part in Italian eating. Fruit is the most frequent way to end an everyday meal; on special days, though, not to have something sweet would be critical. Sarah Cavaliere made more desserts than most and when she wasn't making her well-known apple pie she was turning out her sponge cake—perfectly fluffy and fragrant with vanilla. The cake doesn't want a lot of dressing up, perhaps some sliced very ripe fresh peaches and a little beaten cream.

RAVIOLI WITH RICOTTA AND FRESH TOMATO COMPOTE

About 48 2-inch ravioli, serving 4 to 6

1½ cups unbleached all-purpose flour
2 extra-large eggs, lightly beaten with a fork
1 tablespoon chopped fresh thyme leaves, or 1½ teaspoons dried
 thyme leaves
2 to 3 teaspoons water, if needed
1 cup ricotta cheese
2 egg yolks
6 large basil leaves, rinsed if necessary
½ cup grated good Parmesan cheese
5 tablespoons olive oil
Salt and freshly ground pepper to taste
2 pounds fresh ripe tomatoes, peeled, seeded and diced

Make the ravioli dough either by hand or in a food processor by blending together the flour, whole eggs, 1 teaspoon fresh or ½ teaspoon dried thyme and any water necessary to help the dough form a fine crumbly mixture that is barely moist enough to form a ball. Knead the dough on a lightly floured surface for 2 or 3 minutes; it will be stiff and extremely elastic. If you are using a pasta rolling machine, divide the dough into 6 parts and roll each out into a rectangle; if you are rolling the dough by hand, divide it into 4 and roll each piece on a lightly floured surface into a 12- to 13-inch circle (the dough will be very thin, less than ¹⁄₁₆ of an inch, and will require a certain amount of exertion to achieve that). Dust the rolled out dough lightly with flour and set aside on the work surface to dry out slightly while you make the ricotta filling.

In a food processor or bowl blend together the ricotta, 1 teaspoon fresh or ½ teaspoon dried thyme leaves, the egg yolks, basil leaves (cut into fine strips if you are mixing the ravioli filling by hand), 2 tablespoons of the Parmesan cheese, 1 tablespoon of the olive oil, and salt and pepper to taste. Brush half the sheets of pasta dough with water (it is important that the dough be uniformly moist so that the ravioli will seal properly). Place the ricotta mixture in a pastry bag fitted with a plain ½-inch tip and pipe 1½- to 2-teaspoon bits of ravioli filling about 2 inches apart over the surface of the moistened dough; or simply use a couple of teaspoons to distribute the ricotta mixture. Lay the remaining sheets of dough over the filling and press firmly with your fingers around each bit of filling to seal the ravioli. Cut the ravioli into 2-inch squares using either a knife or a pizza cutter; any pasta trimmings can be dried and saved to put in a *minestrone*. Arrange the ravioli on a couple of baking sheets lined with kitchen towels where they can wait for up to an hour at room temperature, covered with another towel. (The ravioli may also be completed a few hours in advance, covered with plastic wrap and refrigerated.)

Warm the remaining olive oil in a saucepan set over medium-low heat. Add the tomatoes, season with salt and pepper and add the remaining thyme. Stir over the heat just until the tomato mixture is hot; keep warm while you cook the ravioli.

Cook the ravioli in a large quantity of boiling saled water for 1 to 2 minutes; the exact cooking time will depend on the texture of the dough and how much it has dried after being rolled out. Slice off a bit of a ravioli to check for doneness: The pasta should be tender and plump and only faintly chewy. Use a skimmer or slotted spoon to lift the ravioli out of the water and into a colander set over a bowl to drain thoroughly. Arrange the ravioli on a warmed platter or plates, spoon the tomato compote over and then sprinkle with the remaining Parmesan cheese and a little fresh pepper.

GRILLED SALMON WITH BREAD CRUMBS

Serves 6

Salt and freshly ground pepper to taste
6 salmon steaks, about 1 inch thick, brought to room
temperature before cooking
Olive oil
3 cups coarse slightly stale homemade bread crumbs
Wedges of lemon

Season the salmon steaks with salt and pepper and brush them on both sides with a little olive oil. Coat the steaks evenly with the bread crumbs. Place the salmon on a grill set over hot wood-charcoal embers (the coals should be glowing not flaming). Grill the salmon for 2 to 3 minutes on each side, covered with the lid of the barbecue, if you have one, to damp the coals if they seem inclined to flare up; covering the salmon will also impart a smokier flavor to the fish. When the salmon has reached the desired doneness (it is good on the medium-rare side), place it on a warm platter or plates, remove and discard the skin, and, if you wish, the backbone from each steak (which makes 2 pieces out of each). Serve with the wedges of lemon.

NANA SARAH'S SPONGE CAKE

■■■

A 10-inch tube pan for 10 to 12

6 eggs, separated, at room temperature
½ cup cold water
1½ cups sugar
2 teaspoons vanilla extract
1½ cups sifted cake flour
¾ teaspoon cream of tartar
¼ teaspoon salt
Powdered sugar in a shaker or fine sieve

Preheat the oven to 325° F.

With an electric mixer beat the egg yolks until they are thick and lemon colored. Beat the cold water into the yolks, then the sugar and vanilla and continue beating until light and fluffy (this will probably take 6 to 8 minutes at high speed). Gradually fold the flour into the yolk mixture.

Beat the egg whites with the cream of tartar and salt until stiff but not dry. Stir a spoonful of the whites into the yolk mixture to lighten it, then fold the yolk mixture into the remaining whites. Pour into a 10-inch ungreased tube pan and bake for 55 to 60 minutes, until the cake is a golden brown. Cool the cake in the pan on a rack for 20 minutes or so, run a spatula around the sides and unmold the cake onto the rack to finish cooling. Dust with powdered sugar. The sponge cake goes well with fresh fruit salad—very ripe sliced peaches are especially good—and slightly sweetened beaten cream.

23

....

THAT RUTHERFORD
DUST

Rutherford, California

P aris to Rutherford was quite a journey in 1938, but André
Tchelistcheff never flinched. He had heard plenty about the American Wild West and wanted to try it out. Besides, with war on the
way, the City of Lights was growing dimmer by the minute and a
summons to the Golden State was if nothing else a matter of salva-
tion. So one September day the delicately boned young Russian
wine chemist with the gallant smile strode aboard the *Ile de France*
and sailed away to the rich land of California.

The summons had come from the Beaulieu Vineyard of the Napa
Valley, one of the few that was flush from Prohibition (sacramental
wines had boomed when normal wine-making stopped, and booze
went underground, during the bootleg years). Beaulieu's founder,
Georges de Latour, was lord over a carnival collection of fermented
concoctions—every fortified and sweetish wine under the sun, not
to mention some wobbly generic wines—but nothing to call a clear
source of pride. *Except the Cabernet.* Just off the boat, André tasted
that Cabernet at the Beaulieu cellar in New York, and in that taste
his destiny appeared. He had found a wine, already good, at the
start of its journey. From 1938 on they would journey together.

If Rutherford just after Prohibition was rough, André Tchelistcheff was ready. The swaggering locals, and especially the dignified
spirited Mexicans in their sombreros, swirled around the Rutherford

crossroads and cheered André up. And after the rotting fear of Nazi-ascendant France, good cheer suited André just fine. He and his wife and son set up housekeeping in the Yellow Castle, a three-bedroom cottage on the Beaulieu compound, and felt like royalty. André's first endeavor as oenologist at Beaulieu was simple: He tasted every wine. Those wines, and the whole wine-making plant in general, were a mess. Primitive and coarse, the Beaulieu wines, and in fact just about all the California wines in production after Prohibition, were desperate for intervention. It was a pivotal moment: Enter on the scene a radiantly intelligent, cultivated and soulful wine-maker, and the Beaulieu wines, and eventually all of California wine-making, would be changed forever. Naturally neither André nor anyone else knew it at the time. He was just happy to find himself challenged by a free and somewhat crazy new life. As he strolled home at night from the lab to his Castle, the colored lights of the Beaulieu sign made him chuckle, and the lavish, mythical beauty of the Napa Valley breathed all around him and filled him with joy. He had found his home.

Not that there wasn't struggle involved, especially at the start. Fixing a winery is a little like fixing a ballet company. If things look up in five years, it's a wonder; in less than two, call it a miracle. At Beaulieu André was faced with physical chaos and a total lack of philosophy. The plant was decrepit: Barrels were rotting and wines totally out of control, murky and often fermenting in the bottle. In his first two weeks in Rutherford André assessed all of this, succumbed to one brief fit of despair and nearly returned to France. He then just as quickly recovered his senses. California needed him. Also, here he had a powerful winery-owner who was launching him and laying every resource at his feet. His crisis past, embraced by the New World, André plunged in. Within six months a new wine-making plant was under construction, with the concept of extended barrel-aging as its foundation. And—more important than any of that—André walked over the land. Gazing at the grapes, sensing them with his mind and his heart, André knew what he had known in France: To make a great wine he needed a great vineyard. His search was not long. Four blocks of Ranch #1 just south of town had greatness, six inches of it, sitting over the subsoil.

The light Rutherford topsoil challenged the vines and gave the grapes the taste that made the first great red wine of post-Prohibition California: the 1938 Beaulieu Georges de Latour Private Reserve Cabernet Sauvignon, released in 1942. Beaulieu, and California wine-making along with it, emerging from its long-held crouch, under a graceful, knowing touch began a lope that would lengthen to a long sprint. And the colored lights of the Beaulieu sign glowed contentedly at night.

In 1974 another summons from Rutherford reached France. A California red wine—a Beaulieu 1968—had staggered the French in a blind tasting when it eclipsed their prized Bordeaux vintages. A brazen native of Normandy received this news in a totally un-French fashion: She was elated and fascinated. When Simca— Simone Beck, the French coauthor of lustrous books with Julia Child—wrote me this news, I did the only hospitable thing: with my pal Billy Cross I invited her to California to taste this startling red wine and meet the audacious man who had made it. Simca came to Rutherford in the autumn of 1974, and on beholding the Napa splendor was speechless. The clear light and intricate shade, the display of palms and pines and walnut and olive trees, of oleander and begonias and old roses, framing the quiet vines, smote Simca as it had smitten André in 1938. And in the Tchelistcheff wines, and other California wines influenced by him, Simca found the deep taste of mother earth. Simca only came for a month but her stay, also in a yellow house, also altered the Napa Valley. In her uninhibited fashion Simca carried with her the strength and structure and subtle myths of French food, which in the years after roamed over the Napa Valley and all of California, mingling with native values and finding a place with wine in the soil and sun.

When the Old World roots in the New, greatness sometimes grows. The dapper man from France, who arrived in California to shed light with his wines and blaze a trail for others and become a legend of the American West, certainly proved that. So it's natural that people would look at André Tchelistcheff's life and see only heavenly wines. But when André looks at his life in the New World, he sees something else. He loves wine, yes, but he loves something else more, and that is the sight and serenity of the purplish Napa vines.

THAT RUTHERFORD DUST

Individual Onion and Tomato Tarts
with Thyme

Canards à la Margaux (Cold Poached
Duck in Cabernet Aspic)

Tender Greens with Chive Cream
Vinaigrette

Millefeuille de Framboises (Caramelized
Puff Pastry with Raspberries)

———

When I lived and worked in the Napa Valley in the 1970's, there was a kind of cooking that came naturally—rustic, refined, without clutter, it was like the valley was then. Dishes had the depth of wine, the play of herbs, the good cheer of local gardens. Cooking among friends, someone once called it. The menu here is from that time, from a supper I cooked in 1981 to celebrate the marriage of the wine-maker Robert Mondavi—perhaps the greatest Tchelistcheff disciple—to his wife Margrit. The Napa evening was breathless and clear, that night. The food was clearly of France, and the wines of Napa were everywhere—in the goblets, in the duck, in all the flavors of fellowship.

I chose a cold menu for that July evening: one dish with earthy flavors, one dish with rich wine flavors and a dessert with tart berry flavors. To honor the Napa heat, no cream or butter sauces; to honor the Napa wine men, plenty of red wine. The vegetable tart and the duck are both vintage dishes from Simca, who brought them to Napa and left them behind to grow and ripen California-style over the years; they both contain all of her scrupulous dedication to good flavor.

The individual onion and tomato tarts are somewhat rough in appearance, with simple tastes, and this is welcome before the sophistication of the duck and the raspberry dessert. You might wonder why a menu would contain both a first course and a dessert with pastry, but the end results are drastically different, and also, they are separated from each other by a main course that contains no starch whatsoever.

The poached duck in Cabernet is a dish full of the techniques and best tastes of France. As with many involved French dishes, if taken in steps it should not be too formidable a task. The work can certainly be spread over several days: the poaching of the ducks and the clarifying of the aspic done two days before, the liver mousse and boning of the duck done the day following, and the final assembly done the day of serving. The preparation of a meat in aspic dish has a logical progression, centering around its essential component: an initially crude but aromatic broth reinforced with more aromatic ingredients and enhanced with wine, then reduced, clarified, and further refined to its final limpid and delectable state.

The "Margaux" in the title comes from the famous first-growth red wine of Bordeaux, which in the original version of this dish was the only liquid used, and it bled so clear a red throughout the aspic it never needed clarifying. If the dish is balanced, however, with a savory stock as it is here, some clarifying must take place, which is easily done in the classic fashion with egg whites. As for the wine to use, the greater the wine the greater the dish. The duck's luxurious taste is heightened, too, not only by the Cabernet, but by the duck livers, which are sautéed, enriched with butter, perfumed with fresh tarragon, and transformed into a mousse, very reminiscent of *foie gras*, to flavor each piece of duck. Because of the complexity of the duck dish, a simple green salad with no vinegar to disturb the wine flavors is the best accompaniment. A dressing of olive oil, lemon and chives, softened by the addition of a little cream, works well.

The raspberry *millefeuille* does not include a recipe for puff pastry, an intricate dough that is best mastered by consulting a book on French cooking: *Mastering the Art of French Cooking, Volume II*, and *Michel Guérard's Cuisine Gourmande* are excellent sources. If you don't wish to make your own puff pastry, it is generally available frozen in specialty stores and some supermarkets. Keep in mind that making your own can be very satisfying, if only because you will know exactly what it contains. Once you have read the dessert recipe through you may wonder why you even need true-blue puff pastry, since the first thing you do is weigh it down to prevent it from puffing. However, once you have tasted thin golden sheets of caramelized puff pastry you will understand why no other dough will do.

INDIVIDUAL ONION AND TOMATO TARTS WITH THYME

▪▪▪

Serves 6

2 cups unbleached all-purpose flour
Salt and freshly ground pepper to taste
*10 tablespoons cold unsalted butter, cut into 1 to 2 tablespoon
    chunks*
1 whole egg beaten with 1 tablespoon water
½ cup grated Italian Parmesan cheese
½ cup olive oil
2 pounds onions, peeled and sliced
2 tablespoons minced shallots
*2 pounds very ripe flavorful tomatoes, peeled, seeded and
    chopped**
*1 teaspoon finely chopped fresh thyme, or ½ teaspoon dried
    thyme leaves*
1 dozen tiny black niçoise olives, pitted and halved

Working either with a food processor or by hand, stir together the flour and 1 teaspoon salt, then blend in the butter until the mixture has somewhat the texture of oatmeal. Add the beaten egg and stir the dough into a slightly damp ball (if there is any dry mixture left at the bottom of the bowl, mix in a few more drops of water: The dough should be moist, but not sticky, when you poke your finger into the center of the ball). Turn the dough out onto a lightly floured surface and knead a few times. Form the dough into 6 balls and dust them lightly with flour. You may roll the dough out immediately, although if it seems very soft or it is an especially warm day, you may want to wrap it in plastic wrap and chill it for at least ½ hour or for up to 3 or 4 days.

On a lightly floured surface roll out the dough into rounds about 6 inches in diameter and ⅛ inch thick. Place on baking sheets and pinch up the sides to make a small standing edge about ⅓ inch high. Sprinkle a bit of the cheese over the rounds and chill in the freezer for at least 20 minutes. (The pastry may be wrapped and kept frozen for several weeks until ready to use.)

Heat ¼ cup of the olive oil in a large heavy saucepan or skillet, add the onions, season lightly, and stir over medium heat for a minute or two to coat them with the olive oil. Cover the pan and lower the heat; cook the onions for 15 to 20 minutes, stirring them from time to time, until they are nearly tender. Uncover the pan and continue cooking and stirring occasionally until the onions are very tender and sweet—for about 20 to 30 minutes more. Correct the seasoning with salt and pepper.

Place the remaining ¼ cup olive oil in a large deep saucepan set over medium heat. Add the shallots and stir for 2 or 3 minutes to cook them slightly. Stir in the tomatoes, season lightly, and cook, uncovered, for 25 to 30 minutes, until much of the liquid has evaporated and the tomato sauce is thick and fairly smooth. Correct the seasoning and add the thyme.

Preheat the oven to 400° F.

Remove the pastry rounds from the freezer, spread the onions in an even layer over the bottom of each round and sprinkle on a bit more cheese. Divide the tomato sauce among the tarts and spread evenly over the onions. Sprinkle on the remaining cheese and top with the olives in a nice design. Bake for 20 to 25 minutes, until the cheese is lightly browned and the pastry is done. Let cool on a rack at least 20 minutes before serving. The tarts are best served warm or at room temperature; garnish with branches of fresh thyme if you wish.

Note: If no good tomatoes are available, an excellent tomato sauce can be made by combining 4 tablespoons tomato paste mixed with ⅔ cup water or good chicken stock; reduce the simmering time to 15 minutes.

CANARDS À LA MARGAUX
(Cold Poached Duck in Cabernet Aspic)

▪▪▪

Serves 6

3 4- to 5-pound fresh ducks
3 carrots, scrubbed and chopped
3 stalks celery, rinsed and chopped
2 medium onions, peeled and sliced
1 bunch of parsley
Several fresh thyme branches, or 2 teaspoons dried thyme leaves
1 bay leaf
1 cup mirepoix: *equal amounts of finely minced carrots, celery, onions and shallots*
2 bottles good Cabernet or Bordeaux wine
Salt and freshly ground pepper to taste
3 egg whites and the shells
2 or 3 branches fresh tarragon
3 envelopes powdered gelatin
1 pound fresh duck livers
1 stick unsalted butter
1 tablespoon minced shallot
¼ cup good brandy or Armagnac
1 tablespoon chopped fresh tarragon

Remove all extraneous fat from both ends of the ducks. Cut up the birds and whack off the drumstick joint with a cleaver or butt of a heavy knife. Set aside the legs and thighs (kept in one piece) and the breasts. Place the duck backs, necks, gizzards and well-scrubbed feet, if you have them, into a large pot along with the carrots, celery, onions, parsley, thyme and bay leaf. Cover with water and *simmer* for 1½ to 2 hours; do not boil the stock as this will tend to cloud it. Strain the stock discarding the bones and vegetables and degrease it thoroughly. Wash out the pot, return it to the stove, add the *mirepoix* and red wine and boil until reduced by half. Add the duck stock, bring it back to the simmer and add the duck breasts and leg and thigh pieces. Poach the breasts for 15 to 18 minutes, the dark meat for 20 to 25 minutes; as it is done remove the duck meat to a platter to cool. Strain and thoroughly degrease the poaching liquid (if you wish prepare the dish up to this point in advance, cover and refrigerate the duck and the liquid when cool; the stock is easier to degrease when cold). Boil the stock down to 2 quarts and season lightly. Chill 2 cups of stock (stir over ice water to speed it up if you wish).

To clarify the stock, break up the egg whites and shells in a mixing bowl using a whisk or metal spoon (wooden spoons can retain traces of fat or oil which can disrupt the clarifying process). Gradually beat in the 2 cups of chilled stock, then stir the egg white mixture into the remaining liquid; add the tarragon branches, pour into a saucepan and whisk gently over medium heat until the stock is warmed through. Stop beating, and allow the stock to near the simmer undisturbed. As the liquid begins to simmer, lower the heat to maintain a gentle flow of the stock over and through the coagulated egg whites. Egg whites will turn gray as they extract cloudy particles from the liquid. Simmer for 10 minutes or so. Gently ladle the clarified stock through a fine sieve lined with cheesecloth.

Sprinkle the gelatin over ¾ cup cold water. When it has softened, stir it into the hot clarified liquid. Correct the seasoning with salt and pepper, remembering to use sufficient salt to compensate for the loss of savor when the stock is cold. Chill until set. The aspic should be softly gelled (see note at end of recipe).

Pick through the livers, removing any stringy or greenish bits. Melt 4 tablespoons of the butter in a large skillet, add the shallot and stew over low heat for 1 or 2 minutes. Raise the heat to high, add the livers and sauté them for 1 to 1½ minutes; they should remain pink at the center and be slightly soft when pressed with a finger. Pour on the brandy or Armagnac, set alight and flame until the alcohol has evaporated. Season the livers and set aside to cool briefly. Purée the livers in a food processor, then beat in the remaining 4 tablespoons butter, the chopped tarragon and ¼ cup of the set aspic. Correct the seasoning with salt and pepper. Cover and chill.

Pull off all the skin from the pieces of duck; remove the bones from the breast and thighs (the only bone remaining to dress up the dish will be the tidy drumstick bone). Season the meat lightly all over; slice the breasts as thinly as you like. Using a small flexible-blade spatula spread the duck liver mousse lightly over the slices of breast, then reassemble each breast; spread the inside of each thigh with liver mousse. Chill until ready to coat with aspic.

Liquefy 3 cups of the aspic very slightly by stirring momentarily over hot water or very low heat; when ready, the aspic should have a smooth, syrupy quality (if it overliquefies stir over ice water to thicken it again). Using a pastry brush coat the duck pieces with several layers of aspic, chilling the duck in between each application. When the duck in aspic is set (about 50 to 60 minutes), arrange it on a chilled serving platter. Chop the remaining aspic, sprinkled with a few drops of cold water to keep it from sticking to itself, either with a large knife or in a food processor: The chopped aspic pieces should be about the size of corn kernels (the firmer the aspic, the finer you can chop it). Use a pastry bag (no tip is necessary) to pipe the aspic around each piece of duck and over the uncovered spaces on the platter; or, you can simply spoon the aspic all around. Chill until ready to serve. Garnish with sprigs of fresh herbs if you wish.

A note on aspic: An aspic made as described in this recipe—set with the natural gelatin in a homemade stock reinforced with powdered gelatin—will have a lovely melting quality when eaten but will be a little tricky to handle, especially in very warm weather when it will tend to liquefy fairly rapidly. If you wish a sturdier aspic, increase the amount of powdered gelatin to 4 envelopes, which meets the standard formula of 1 envelope for every 2 cups of liquid. Before doing this, you might want to test the aspic by chilling a small amount and checking its consistency, since the gelatin in the duck bones alone may have given enough additional body to the stock.

TENDER GREENS WITH CHIVE CREAM VINAIGRETTE

■■

Serves 6

2 to 3 teaspoons lemon juice
¼ cup good olive oil
2 teaspoons chopped fresh chives
1 to 2 tablespoons heavy cream
½ to ¾ teaspoon salt
Freshly ground pepper to taste
¾ to 1 pound washed tender salad greens

If you wish to make the vinaigrette in advance, do so by combining the lemon juice, oil, chives, cream and seasonings either in a blender or in a bowl with a whisk. Or, you may simply add the ingredients for the dressing to the greens and toss just before serving.

Note: Because of the variables involved in making a good salad—the pungence of the oil, the tartness of the lemons, the type of greens—and because salad tastes are so personal anyway, I have allowed a range in the quantities of ingredients.

MILLEFEUILLE DE FRAMBOISES
(Caramelized Puff Pastry with Raspberries)

■■

Serves 6

1½ pounds chilled puff pastry
Powdered sugar in a shaker
1 quart fresh raspberries
¾ cup sugar
1 cup heavy cream
1 teaspoon vanilla extract
Sprigs of fresh mint

Preheat the oven to 425° F.

Divide the puff pastry in half. On a lightly floured surface roll each piece into a rectangle about 8 inches wide and 18 inches long; the pastry will be quite thin, about ¹⁄₁₆ inch thick. Place each piece of pastry on a baking sheet and prick all over with a fork, then place another baking sheet over the pastry (for this particular use of puff pastry, you do not want the dough to rise but to remain thin while it bakes and becomes brown and very crisp). Bake for 5 or 6 minutes. Remove the top baking sheets and continue baking for another 15 to 18 minutes, or until the pastry is golden brown. Remove from the oven; turn the oven to broil and place a rack in the middle of the oven. Sprinkle one of the pieces of puff pastry evenly and quite heavily with powdered sugar and set on the rack under the broiler for 30 seconds to 1 minute, depending on the heat of your broiler. The sugar will melt, turn clear, then caramelize within a matter of seconds; remove the pastry from the oven *the instant it has caramelized* (leaving the pastry under the broiler for even a few seconds too long can produce a burned mess, so you must watch the pastry the entire time it is under the broiler). Set on a rack to cool and repeat with the remaining piece of pastry. You now have 2 pieces of crisp puff pastry with a delicious caramel seal that also waterproofs it from the damp filling.

Pick through the raspberries and try to refrain from washing them (which only dilutes their flavor). Place 3½ cups of the berries in a bowl and mash them with a fork. Just before serving sweeten the berries to taste, about ½ cup sugar should be enough; the beauty of this dessert is achieved by having the courage to leave the berries tart. Beat the cream with the remaining ¼ cup sugar and the vanilla until it has enough body to hold its shape but is not really stiff.

Place the 2 pieces of puff pastry on top of each other and trim the edges with a serrated knife to make 2 equal rectangles. Place one piece of pastry, caramel side up, on a cutting surface. Spread the cream evenly over the pastry, then spoon the raspberry compote over the cream. Place the other piece of pastry over the dessert, caramel side up. Using a serrated knife, slice the *millefeuille* into 6 portions. With the help of a large spatula, transfer the pastries to a large serving platter. Garnish with the remaining raspberries and the sprigs of mint. Dust the dessert—pastry, garnishes, the edges of the platter—generously with sieved powdered sugar and serve.

The *millefeuille* can also be assembled on the serving platter, garnished, presented whole, then sliced at the table. This is a rather more impressive handling of the dessert, requiring an extra bit of composure to slice it in public. Either way—sliced in the kitchen or at the table—don't fret if the slices aren't perfect. The pastry is fragile, the cream soft, and the berries juicy—slightly precarious to serve but luscious to eat.

24

....

OLD GOLD HILLS

Goodyears Bar, California

Y ou won't do much drinking in Goodyears Bar. It's a real bar all right, a sandbar, about a quarter mile below Goodyears Bridge. And the good stuff that flows there is called the Yuba River. Goodyears Bar is an old mining town in the high Sierras of California and now a very still place. Even the heat has a hush. On most summer days all you'll hear is the wind in the woods, floating over the sound of water.

I was eight years old my first summer in Goodyears Bar. We stayed in the Red House, at the end of the one empty street. That street followed the river, and where the river bent right, the road bent left and there you had the Red House. We loved that funny mountain house. It had a bathroom with three doors, lumpy floors, fat and skinny spiders, and a low black wood stove that lumbered along one whole kitchen wall and roared like a locomotive when it was fired up (even on summer mornings you wanted that fire). There were four kids and magic in the Red House that summer of '58.

We made two friends right away in Goodyears Bar. The first was the river. From the Red House to the Bend was a five-minute slither over rocks and creeks and, at the very last, past the high "bee weeds" which we'd race through hoping the bees wouldn't notice. That last bit of bravery was always worthwhile, because the river was there waiting. In those years the Bend was the town swimming hole, and

303

it was perfect. It was deep and shallow and fast and slow. Most of the town—fifteen or twenty people or so—turned out for those summer afternoons at the river. It was kind of like a swim social. There was always Doreen Quinn, who was thin thin, but who'd dip her bones in the chilly river, then settle on her towel laid on the gravely beach and pull deeply on her Pall Malls. Into her seventies and comfortably padded, Sidney Strand was older and kindly and she did a beautiful calm crawl. She just glided along. Broad-shouldered Bette Bishop and her kids, Vernon, Joe and Jessie, usually showed up too but Bette would always rather talk and smoke than swim—and she could light a match with her thumbnail. As for me, a shy, skinny city kid, the Yuba River and my mom taught me not just to swim but also not to be afraid. The river had scared me at first, but then I learned to trust it and to love it. So we would all gather there, the summer people and the locals, on the shore of the Yuba, to swim and howl in the cold water (although in August it always eased up some), then laze and warm up in the sun and feel the slow hours of summer drift by.

The second friend we made was Winnie McCrindle. She lived next to the Red House in another funny wooden house with a steep tin roof. Winnie was sixty-something and tiny, shy of five feet, with short white hair and the pink skin of a baby. She kept her skin soft and smooth with Lava soap and Mennen Skin Bracer. That's how Winnie was in life—rough stuff never made her rough, it made her gentle. Growing up in the back woods of Washington and California around 1910 with a drifting dad and a diabetic mom was no bed of roses, but Winnie always found a way to laugh. She didn't mind a childhood living on beans and "thick soups" (stews with more vegetables than meat) and traveling in a horse-and-wagon, because along the way she learned her love of the woods.

As Winnie's neighbors that long ago summer we learned her love of the woods too. When we could be dragged away from the river, one sister or another and I went with Winnie and our mom prospecting for gold. Gold was still there in the streams of the Sierras, and Winnie usually found it. She didn't use a pan or any fancy sluice, she just ranged over the rocks along the creek patiently nudging the nameless gray stone to reveal the pale quartz where the gold liked to cling. Winnie didn't say much as she eyed the terrain; you might have thought she was listening to the stones. I stared at a lot of rocks and I never found any gold, but the forest was alive and still and that was just as good. At the end of a morning, gold or no gold, Winnie would haul home her favorite rocks and put them under her bed.

Winnie Grovenburgh McCrindle was a mountain woman first, last and always. The person they called the female Daniel Boone wouldn't have had any idea what to do in a city. Her whole life had to do with the woods. Chopping wood, whittling willow branches with the kids, building primitive pine furniture, and also, looking for that last rock—that was what she knew. She could also barber hair. She'd barbered her father and brothers and the sawmill workers in Graniteville in the early thirties, standing in rain puddles that in winter collected at the barbering end of her slanted cabin floor (one of the men once begged Winnie for a tooth-pull along with the haircut, which she gave but not before she'd gotten the logger good and liquored up). So naturally, Winnie barbered us kids too. When we met Winnie she was married to a Scot named Shorty McCrindle; Winnie was probably the only woman he could stand next to and not earn that name. Coming from the strangely cultured atmosphere of Berkeley as we did, we loved those peaceable loving mountain folk. They were kind, and when we were with them, we were mountain folk too.

The only place you never saw Winnie was down at the river. All that cold water spooked her. Ask Winnie to hunt bear and she'd have her big gun tucked in her pants and be out the door before you could blink. Now, no one really remembered Winnie ever shooting a bear; she sure liked to track 'em though. But get in that river? She'd as soon have snuggled up to a rattlesnake. Winnie hated cold. Even on the hottest summer days she had her uniform: a thick flannel shirt, tight-buttoned at her wrists and at her throat, with a snug neckerchief just in case. With bad memories of the croup, you didn't fool around with cold.

The river might have been a fearsome or cold place for some, but what came out of the river everyone loved: fresh brook trout. The McCrindle trout breakfasts were famous. The first day of trout season the McCrindle kids and grandkids would run down to the river at six o'clock and catch ten trout. They'd clean the fish right there, then take them to Winnie and she'd cook them for breakfast, fresh as you could get. There would be mushrooms from the woods sometimes, cooked in butter, and Winnie would always put on a pot of her buckeroo potatoes and stacks of watery pancakes, a McCrindle specialty. The taste of mountain food—plain and soft and smoky—over the years became for me the deep taste of summer.

Goodyears Bar is still a summer place. And it's still perfect. When I walk that same empty summer street that follows the river, the hollyhocks still do their deep bends, and the Red House stands over to the left except it's not red anymore. We don't stay there anyway, after three summers in the Red House my family bought a house up Goodyears Creek. Winnie and Shorty and even Mrs. Strand are still in Goodyears Bar; they rest now on the hill behind the flume, new arrivals among the old dry graves. Every July or August I stop there to greet them and others—Lawrence Gregory, Carl Durrett and his son Rodger—the friends of thirty summers.

And there are still the afternoons at the river. The ritual of the Bend passed into myth one winter when the river ran high and hard and the Bend shifted and then was gone. So I go to the Cliffs now, down from the old Bend, and I have the swimming hole mostly to myself. I guess fewer folks want that cold water now. Also, the Cliffs is a little far from town. But it has something the Bend never did: the late-in-the-day sun.

OLD GOLD HILLS

Brook Trout Fried in Butter
with Forest Mushrooms

Buckeroo Potatoes

Watery Pancakes

Buttery Blackberry Syrup

Diane Rollins' Fresh Applesauce Cake

Camp Coffee

———

Mountain food, like a lot of plain cooking, tastes best when it's eaten close by. When food has little adornment, proximity to the source of the ingredients means everything. Real freshwater trout, for instance, have a clean and delicate taste and are really the only trout worth eating; farm-raised trout have that murky flavor. So if you aren't near a cold mountain stream where you can reel 'em in yourself, just eat something else. The same goes for the blackberries. Wild blackberries you pick yourself in August have a flavor you can never find in market berries. The buttery syrup is fine without any berries at all—raspberries or boysenberries would overwhelm the gentle maple flavor; only wild blackberries, with their cool, slightly smoky flavor, really blend calmly with the syrup.

If you do make the trout with wild mushrooms, of course you can use any flavorful, and safe, wild mushroom that you gather in the woods or perhaps more prudently find in the market. The McCrindle bunch used to bring home bolete mushrooms, a mushroom with pores rather than gills. Along with the mushrooms, the buckeroo potatoes, a soft, not crisp, breakfast potato, are a good accompaniment to the tender trout.

Watery pancakes, a real McCrindle specialty, were so popular with the grandkids (who named them) that they used to cluster around the stove and grab the first ones that came off the griddle. They are in fact nothing more than very thin pancakes, with a little cornmeal added for texture, that cook to a rich lacy brown. You can eat lots of them and still have room for fresh applesauce cake.

BROOK TROUT FRIED IN BUTTER WITH FOREST MUSHROOMS

....

Serves 6

Salt and freshly ground pepper to taste
6 fresh trout, 10 to 14 ounces each, cleaned, rinsed and patted
    dry
Flour on a plate for dredging
6 tablespoons butter
¾ pound wild mushrooms, thoroughly rinsed and dried, stems
    trimmed—halved or quartered or sliced, depending on the
    size and type
2 teaspoons chopped fresh thyme, or 1 teaspoon dried thyme
    leaves
Lemon wedges

Salt and pepper each trout, roll in the flour and pat with your hands to remove any excess. Place 2 large skillets over medium-high heat. Add 2 tablespoons butter to each pan and when it is foaming and hot add the trout. Cook for 1½ to 2 minutes on each side, until just done (the trout should just begin to flake off the bone). Remove to a platter and keep warm.

Melt the remaining 2 tablespoons butter in one of the skillets. Add the mushrooms and cook them over high heat until they are tender, stirring or tossing frequently. Season the mushrooms and add the thyme. Arrange the mushrooms over and around the trout and serve with the lemon wedges.

BUCKEROO POTATOES

Serves 6

8 strips of bacon
1 onion, peeled and sliced
Salt and freshly ground pepper to taste
2 pounds Russet potatoes, unpeeled but scrubbed, then thinly
  sliced
1½ cups water
½ cup coarsely chopped parsley

Cook the bacon until crisp; drain on absorbent paper, and reserve 2 tablespoons of the bacon fat. Crumble the bacon when it is cool.

Heat the reserved bacon fat in a large heavy pot or skillet; stir in the onion, season lightly, cover and cook over medium-low heat for 8 to 10 minutes, stirring occasionally. Remove the lid, add the bacon, potatoes and water. Add a little more salt and pepper. Cover the pan once again and cook gently for 20 to 25 minutes, stirring or tossing every now and then (don't worry if some of the slices break). When the potatoes are very tender, remove the lid and reduce the liquid, if necessary, until only a few tablespoons remain. Correct the seasoning with salt and pepper. Stir in the parsley and serve.

WATERY PANCAKES

■■

Serves 4 to 6

1 cup unbleached all-purpose flour
1/4 cup cornmeal
3/4 teaspoon baking soda
1/2 teaspoon baking powder
1/4 teaspoon salt
1 tablespoon sugar
1 cup buttermilk
3/4 cup milk
1/4 cup water
1 egg, lightly beaten
2 tablespoons corn oil (or other tasteless oil) and oil for the
    griddle

In a mixing bowl stir together the dry ingredients. With a fork or whisk mix together the liquid ingredients, then beat gently into the dry mixture, mixing only until well moistened (if there are small lumps, it's fine). Let the batter sit for 10 to 15 minutes, to allow the flour and cornmeal to absorb the liquid. Pour a thin coating of oil on a griddle or a couple of large skillets set over medium-high heat. When the cooking surface is hot pour on 2 or 3 tablespoons of batter to form each pancake. Cook for 1 or 2 minutes, until nicely browned, then brown lightly on the other side. Keep the pancakes warm in the oven while you continue to make pancakes with the rest of the batter. Serve with the buttery blackberry syrup (recipe follows).

BUTTERY BLACKBERRY SYRUP

■■■

For 1½ cups

½ cup maple syrup
2 tablespoons butter
1 cup very ripe wild blackberries

Place the syrup and butter in a small saucepan and heat to a gentle boil. Whisk or stir for 30 seconds or so at the simmer to incorporate the butter. Add the blackberries and stir for a moment or two, just to warm the berries and allow them to soften and release some of their juice. Serve warm or at room temperature with the pancakes.

DIANE ROLLINS' FRESH APPLESAUCE CAKE

■■■

A 2-quart loaf pan for 10

1 cup thick unsweetened homemade applesauce
1 teaspoon baking soda
1 teaspoon cinnamon
½ teaspoon ground cloves
½ cup butter at room temperature
1 cup sugar
2 eggs, lightly beaten
1¾ cups flour
¼ teaspoon salt
1 cup raisins
1 cup walnuts, coarsely chopped

Preheat the oven to 350° F.

Warm the applesauce in a small saucepan; add the soda and spices. Cream the butter and sugar until the mixture is fluffy. Stir in the eggs, then the applesauce. Sift together the flour and salt and add to the butter and apple mixture, stirring until smooth. Add the raisins and walnuts. Turn the batter into a lightly buttered 2-quart loaf pan. Bake for 1 hour to 1 hour and 5 minutes; cool on a rack. Serve warm with coffee or tea.

READING LIST
AND SOURCES

Beard, James. *American Cookery*. Boston 1972.

Beck, Simone. *Simca's Cuisine*. New York 1972.

Child, Julia, Louisette Bertholle and Simone Beck. *Mastering the Art of French Cooking*. New York 1961.

Child, Julia, and Simone Beck. *Mastering the Art of French Cooking*. Volume II. New York 1970.

Cunningham, Marion. *The Fannie Farmer Baking Book*. New York 1984.

Cunningham, Marion. *The Fannie Farmer Cookbook*. 13th Edition. New York 1990.

Flagg, Fannie. *Fried Green Tomatoes at the Whistle Stop Cafe*. New York 1987.

Hazan, Marcella. *The Classic Italian Cookbook*. New York 1973.

Guérard, Michel. *Michel Guérard's Cuisine Gourmande*. New York 1979.

Smith, Madeline Babcock. *The Lemon Jelly Cake*. Boston 1952.

ACKNOWLEDGMENTS

I thank:

Marlene Sorosky, Dee Hardie, Carleton Jones and Rob Casper for putting me on the trail of the young Wallis Warfield; Joe Simpson for assisting me in the search for Duchess of Windsor recipes and for his steady presence at the *Baltimore Sun*.

Peter Manning and his chums, Dodie and George, for one of the happiest days I spent on Long Island; Sandra Brown for the pies and Patsy Cline sing-alongs that kept us going all through the Bridgehampton summer; Barney Corrigan, for saying "write, only write," which gave me the will, then the desire to do just that.

Mark DeVoto for his extreme generosity in drawing me into his family history and for those priceless transcripts; Lindy and Bob Barlow for a wonderful evening together cooking and eating Indiana style; Joe Middleton and Lee Barnes for escorting the Simca motorcade of '79 through Louisiana and Mississippi and introducing us to true Southern hospitality, not to mention hilarity; Bettina and Bob Barnes, whose welcome to Natchez could not have been more genuinely gracious; Mel Dick for invaluable assistance with reminiscences and photographs of Patsy Cline.

Mary Brown, for much much remembrance: for taking me, with words, home to Texas; Jane Schroyer, for confirming that the tastes of that Tory summer will never fade; Hal "The Pal" Harron who always lives up to her nickname; Donna Gulley for conveying so patiently the flavors of Wyoming; Emily Crumpacker, who jitterbugs like no one else on either side of the Atlantic; Beck, for keeping the Gig Fub Club alive; Ron Pittman, who feeds a mob at the McCleary Bear Festival with great aplomb.

André Tchelistcheff, quiet prince, who sired a royal line of California wines and wine-makers; Dorothy Tchelistcheff, bright, energetic and sensible woman who helped give the prince long life; Rosemary Rogan Thompson, Sam Matheny, John Luther and Jack Canfield for the depth, humor and candor of their recollections; Turie and Frank, for keeping Italian talent alive down on Wharf #1; Diane and Cy Rollins, whose home on Goodyears Creek is always a place of good eating and good fun.

Iris Linares for her ability, both keen and quiet, to soothe an author's flusters and return him to good cheer; Roger and Phyllis Lapham, for understanding *l'amour du métier*; Leonard Brill for guiding me on the subject of wild mushrooms.

Barbara Lemerman, who twenty-five years ago drew me spellbound into the preparation of our first veal Prince Orloff, which changed me forever; Sydel and Ray Lemerman, for fueling the debate in favor of this book's title, and for making their home always a home to me too.

Jock Soto, for his first trusting appearance—barefoot and smiling—in the kitchen in East Hampton, and for his transfixing panther presence on the State Theater stage; Carmen Ferragano, guardian angel who helped me experience New York as an expansive and supportive place; Cynthia Gregory, for the magnificence of any night she put even one toe on a stage; Constantine and Marcelle Gregory for the loveliness of long friendship and many happy journeys backstage; Matthew Spady, a rogue with tulips; Richard Secrist, for the Chopin.

Steven Ross and Courtney Sale Ross for their incredible attentiveness and generosity, and for two of the most thrilling years of my life.

Maureen and Eric Lasher, tenacious literary agents and good souls, who tracked me down in New York and said "We want you!" making me a very happy fella.

Nyce Jolay for her right-now radiance which, fog or no fog, shines over Monterey Bay. Brian Barlow, stalwart and loving friend, who joined me on the *Slow Food* research tour of 1990 and kept us laughing and expectant every inch of the way; who initiated me into the life of Indiana; and who, back home in Monterey, on a daily basis cheered me on to write my book. His spirit is abundant in these pages; I miss him greatly.

Akiko Matsuo, whose cold lemon soufflé and cream whipped with chopsticks are without equal. David McCorkle, for swan leaps out of a stockpot.

Margrit Biever and Robert Mondavi for demonstrating, when it was 100° in the Napa Valley shade, that Cabernet on the rocks is never uncouth.

Julia Child, for writing me to "get yourself over to France young man and apprentice yourself to the best chef you can find!"; and for that collapsing *Charlotte Chantilly* (which got the letters going).

Françoise de Meaulne, loving French aunt, who welcomed me to France then pointed the way to Simca's door, just around the corner.

Arlette and Robert Glaënzer for drawing me out of my student life in Paris and into the enchantment and delicate flavors of the Loire Valley.

Catherine Jacquard, for gallantry over the garage at the Moulin Brosse.

Shoshanah Dobry who saved the day and sent the cable that said "Stay in France." Axel Fabre, for the dusky silvery clasp of Marrakech.

Yannick Vincent, graceful next to greatness.

Kenneth and Janet Wolfe, Gaston and Colette Lenôtre and their family, the late Jean Troisgros, Pierre and Olympe Troisgros, Michel and Christine Guérard, Roger and Denise Vergé—great chefs, artists, keepers of the flame.

Adrienne and Martin Zausner, who have cooked up *la cuisine de l'amitié* for years; Gael Greene, "*grande blonde aux yeux* no candy."

Audrey Hepburn for her "heaven-reaching neck," and for teaching us all so beguilingly how to crack an egg; Hilda Hensley, for raising so devotedly one of the great American singers.

Renata Alafi, who loved a good dinner and didn't hesitate a second to serve quail in grape sauce while we watched *The Birds*.

Nina Schneyer, Carol Worsley, Ailene Berrard, Harriet Healy, Maizie Newman, Mary Helen DeLong, Ley Zeff, Clara Novoletti, Jane Benet: true-blue one and all.

Maria-Chiara Zanolli, who fed pure Italy to the North Beach Christmas of '73; Monique Brossier, who said "*C'est pouf, Madame*," to Simca and lived to tell it; Gene Opton for the absorbing equipping world of The Kitchen; Jean Gates Hall, for sunny scenes of the yellow house in Rutherford; Bill Henn, lord in the land of Petit Château; Vera Haywood, for circles of peace; Faviana Olivier, for reaching from 1850 over to 1855; Linda Kaye Rogers, who put the worth into Fort Worth; Debra Bronstein, for green tomato good times.

Catherine Brandel, for noticing about the garlic. Margaret Fox, for giving me bread-class biceps.

Lucille McKenzie Cross and Bill "Buddy" Cross, for comfort and togetherness over many wonderful years on Lochinvar Avenue.

Edna Mae Austin, for prince employment for one magical week.

Amy Rutherford, my sixth-grade teacher at Oxford Elementary School who first taught me about excellence.

Margaret Gregory and Feather Ortiz, who helped keep me on the line from Goodyears Bar to New York City.

E.M., for hope and eloquence; Mary Challans, who, too, is Alexander.

Madeleine Haas Russell, for that companionable evening of recollections near the beautiful hearth of the Atherton house.

Deborah Beggs Moncrief, who knows beauty and helps create it; who understands talent and supports it.

Lurline Matson Roth, grand spirit who well into her nineties never failed to ask, "What have I got for lunch?"

James Jacob Hege, for "Pie Memories" and the stroll home from *Maurice*; David Lynch, royalty on the job and off; Doug Dickinson, who made the film flicker bright; Michael Manwaring, whose pencil soars. James Rejón, for ruddy smiles; Lee Hayward, for rollin' on the river; Franco Trudu, *amico di lusso*; Richard Sparks, for the glory years in Box R; Michael Thorburn, for pool-house nocturnes.

Ericka Pillars, Dick Dillingham, Arlene Repetto, jj wilson, Marie-Claire Vallois, Ralph Johnson—who love good language. Jerome Frazer, Penelope Johnson, Susan Perry Sotirkos, Mary Ruud Wood, Stanley Holden, Margaret Hills, Michael Vernon, Nanette Glushak, Fran Spector, Sally Streets, Jack Einheber—who love beautiful movement. Symeta Kuper, who loved beautiful music.

Liv Blumer, one-in-a-million editor and friend to an unorthodox book project which she guided—calmly, intelligently, determinedly, and with unextinguishable personal style and humor—through tangents and detours that inevitably led, under her warm direction, to the land of good sense.

Marion Cunningham, who always pumps plenty of high octane into her pals' lives and who also knows better than anyone that labradors (along with sugar) are right up there with oxygen.

Rick O'Connell for the refuge of Junipero Serra Street and for the dog-tired oatmeal suppers at midnight that always tasted as good as any champagne and caviar.

Jeannette Costeiu who, in the Michigan winter of 1973, fishtailed into the parking lot in a gray Corvette, slid down a frigid walkway and into cooking class in a gray fox jacket to make *quenelles sauce suprême*, then stayed to become a lifelong friend.

Teresa Garcia, who put the pride of Mexico into American pie.

Peter Allen and Gregory Cannell for high rockin' times at Radio City. Harvey Milk and Scott Smith whose Castro Camera radiated goodness to neighbors.

Juan Diego Michel, handsome Mexican *caballero*, whose spirit gallops along the peaks of his beloved Jalisco.

Frances Dinkelspiel Green, one of the great California women: compassionate, bold, giving.

Blanca and Babbu, for their perfect appetites and joyous companionship.

My beautiful sisters Polly, Catherine and Barbara, who stand by me always.

My grandfather Emmanuel Vlamis, who cooked me delicious things with great love when I was a child.

My especial gratitude is expressed to Madhur Jaffrey for her readiness to ponder prospects and always guide me to the best ones; for drawing me into the fascinations of her life, involving Delhi and Cannes, New York City and Hillsdale. I thank Madhur most deeply for her constancy; there is no better friend.

I thank profoundly and devotedly my great friend and hero Simca who in 1971 strode into her Paris drawing room and, seeing more than a young man with long hair, heard my best classroom French, then ushered me into the beauty and valor of her world—which I inhabited for many splendid years.

And I thank Billy Cross, for so much, for so long. I thank him mightily for the treasure of Queen Esther, but mostly for just being the barman at the Chez Panisse café, one September day.

PHOTO CAPTIONS

Page v. My parents and sister, Polly
Petersham, Massachusetts, 1943

Page 7. The ballast: Blanca and Babbu, 1988
PHOTOGRAPHER: *Bee Wee Vlamis*

Page 23. Madhur Jaffrey in "Autobiography of a Princess"
London, 1973
Courtesy of Merchant Ivory Productions

Page 37. Avis DeVoto and Julia Child
Paris, 1956
PHOTOGRAPHER: *Paul Child*

Page 49. Wallis Warfield in her junior year at Oldfields School
Glencoe, Maryland, circa 1912
Courtesy of Oldfields School

Page 59. Patsy Cline in the Shenandoah Apple Blossom Parade with
the Melody Playboys
Winchester, Virginia, 1955
Photo contributed by Mel Dick

Page 71. Munnie Rogan and her brood at Oakencroft
Glendale, Ohio, 1950

Page 83. Me and Uncle Bob
Walnut Flat, Kentucky, 1990
PHOTOGRAPHER: *Brian Barlow*

Page 95. Commander E. L. Bud Tucker (*left*) who fed Joe Middleton
(*right*) his first artichoke (*mysterious seaman in center*)
Pearl Harbor, Honolulu, Hawaii, circa 1969

Page 107. The Queen of Spit and Run (Lee Barnes)
Natchez, Mississippi, circa 1958
PHOTOGRAPHER: *Bettina Barnes*

Page 121. The Ardeneaux bunch (*left to right*): Leroy, Mary, George
Houston, Texas, circa 1931

Page 137. Buddy Cross with Billy and Jimmy
Chautauqua Springs, Kansas, 1948
PHOTOGRAPHER: *Lucille McKenzie Cross*

Page 149. Cake royalty: Madeline Babcock Smith, author of
The Lemon Jelly Cake
New York City, early 1950s
PHOTOGRAPHER: *Lotti Jacobi*

Page 159. Brian Barlow: primed for Peanut Hill
Shelbyville, Indiana, 1964

Page 171. Eyes full of cake: John Luther
Springfield, Ohio, circa 1970
PHOTOGRAPHER: *Cese Luther*

Page 181. John's Cadillac (not the La Salle) and Jeannette, parked
at the Highway Market
Royal Oak, Michigan, circa 1953
PHOTOGRAPHER: *Valeria Costeiu*

Page 195. Aunt Betty and Larry Beckwith
Davenport, Iowa, 1958

Page 209. Hal the Pal at Harronerb Farm
Huot, Minnesota, 1989
PHOTOGRAPHER: *Brian Harron*

Page 225. Little Jack Canfield eyeing the open road
Torrington, Wyoming, circa 1945

Page 235. Emily Crumpacker and Gagi at Neahkahnie Beach
Oregon, circa 1960
PHOTOGRAPHER: *Ann Winkler Crumpacker*

Page 247. The Gig Fub Club: Mike and Beck
Goodyears Bar, California, 1989
PHOTOGRAPHER: *Bee Wee Vlamis*

Page 257. Young California beauty: portrait of Marion Cunningham
by Wade Zint
Laguna Beach, California, 1945

Page 273. Turie with octopus
Wharf #1, Monterey, California, 1989

Page 285. André Tchelistcheff in the Beaulieu lab
Rutherford, California, circa 1948

Page 301. Winnie McCrindle, female Daniel Boone
The Sierra Nevada of California, 1935

Page 306. Blanca and Babbu at the Cliffs
North Yuba River   Goodyears Bar, California, 1991
PHOTOGRAPHER: *Michael James*

CONVERSION CHART

LIQUID MEASURES

Fluid Ounces	U.S. Measures	Imperial Measures	Milliliters
	1 tsp.	1 tsp.	5
¼	2 tsp.	1 dessert spoon	7
½	1 T.	1 T.	15
1	2 T.	2 T.	28
2	¼ cup	4 T.	56
4	½ cup or ¼ pint		110
5		¼ pint or 1 gill	140
6	½ cup		170
8	1 cup or ½ pint		225

SOLID MEASURES

U.S. and Imperial Measures		Metric Measures	
Ounces	Pounds	Grams	Kilos
1		28	
2		56	
3½		100	
4	½	112	
5		140	
6		168	
8	½	225	

OVEN TEMPERATURE EQUIVALENTS

Fahrenheit	Gas Mark	Celsius	Heat of Oven
225	¼	107	Very Cool
250	½	121	Very Cool
275	1	135	Cool
300	2	148	Cool
325	3	163	Moderate
350	4	177	Moderate
375	5	190	Fairly Hot

Liquid Measures

fl oz	cups / pints	pints	ml
9			250 (¼ liter)
10	1¼ cups	½ pint	280
12	1½ cups or ¾ pint		340
15		¾ pint	420
16	2 cups or 1 pint		450
18	2¼ cups		500 (½ liter)
20	2½ cups	1 pint	560
24	3 cups or 1½ pints		675
25		1¼ pints	700
27	3½ cups		750
30	3¾ cups	1½ pints	840
32	4 cups or 2 pints or 1 quart		900
35		1¾ pints	980
36	4½ cups		1000 (1 liter)

fl oz	pints	ml	liters
9		250	¼
12	¾	340	
16	1	450	
18	1¼	500	½
20	1½	560	
24		675	
27		750	¾
28	1¾	780	
32	2	900	
36	2¼	1000	1
40	2½	1100	
48	3	1350	
54		1500	1½

Oven Temperatures

°F	Gas Mark	°C	
400	6	204	Fairly Hot
425	7	218	Hot
450	8	232	Very Hot
475	9	246	Very Hot

INDEX

329